Juvenile Court

A Judge's Guide for Young Adults and Their Parents

Leora Krygier

THE SCARECROW PRESS, INC.
Lanham, Maryland • Toronto • Plymouth, UK
2009

SCARECROW PRESS, INC.

Published in the United States of America
by Scarecrow Press, Inc.
A wholly owned subsidiary of
The Rowman & Littlefield Publishing Group, Inc.
4501 Forbes Boulevard, Suite 200, Lanham, Maryland 20706
www.scarecrowpress.com

Estover Road
Plymouth PL6 7PY
United Kingdom

British Library Cataloguing in Publication Information Available

Library of Congress Cataloging-in-Publication Data
Krygier, Leora.
Juvenile court : a judge's guide for young adults and their parents / Leora Krygier.
p. cm.
Includes index.
ISBN-13: 978-0-8108-6127-5 (cloth : alk. paper)
ISBN-10: 0-8108-6127-5 (cloth : alk. paper)
ISBN-13: 978-0-8108-6352-1 (ebook)
ISBN-10: 0-8108-6352-9 (ebook)
1. Juvenile courts–United States. 2. Juvenile delinquency–United States.
I. Title.
KF9795.K79 2009
345.73'081–dc22 2008032075

™ The paper used in this publication meets the minimum requirements of American National Standard for Information Sciences—Permanence of Paper for Printed Library Materials, ANSI/NISO Z39.48-1992.
Manufactured in the United States of America.

For my parents,
Yael and Levi Galperin

Contents

Acknowledgments		vii
Why I Wrote This Guide		ix
Disclaimer		xiii
1	The Juvenile Court System	1
2	I Received a Citation to Court: What Do I Do?	9
3	Preparing for Court	25
4	Coming to Court for My Hearing	45
5	Driving, Pedestrian, Bicycle, and Related Violations	61
6	Other Offenses	89
7	What Can I Expect at Court?	121
8	Returning to Court, the DMV, and Will I Have a Record?	141
9	How to Avoid Getting Another Citation	149
Resources on the Web		155
Glossary		157
Appendix: Document Examples		165
Index		175
About the Author		181

Acknowledgments

Thank you to the wonderful members of my writing group—authors Carolyn Howard-Johnson, Joey Crawford, and Phyllis Gebauer—who have supported and nurtured me and my writing.

Thank you to my staff at the Los Angeles Superior Court—Alicia Nunez, Loretta Holt, Brenda Arana, Mike Scholl, and Kevin Kader—without whom I couldn't begin to do my job.

Thank you to my good friend, author Bob Stone, for his encouragement and generous input and for being the best of pals.

Thank you to my children, Oren and Talia, and husband, David, for being my constant cheerleaders.

And a final thank you to all the teens who've appeared before me over the years. Sharing your stories and your lives has made me a better person and judge.

Why I Wrote This Guide

When I told my daughter I wanted to write a guide specifically for teens about juvenile laws and courts, the first thing she said was, "Why would you want to do that? Isn't that like pulling back the curtain on the Wizard of Oz?" In some ways, she was right. The mystique of juvenile court is part of its power. Although the court is sometimes lightheartedly referred to as "Juvie" court, to a teen facing a court hearing, the unfamiliar procedure, the closed sessions, and even the configuration of the hearing room make for an aura of gravity and apprehension. So why did I want to write this guide? The answer to my daughter's question wasn't immediately apparent to me.

During the fifteen years I've spent as a juvenile court judge, I've had every teen imaginable appear before me: teens with two parents, single parents, and gay parents; teens raised by grandparents, in foster homes, and group homes; average kids and geniuses who had skipped high school; gang kids and taggers; teens whose parents were in jail; and celebrity teens represented by high-powered attorneys. I saw fourteen-year-olds who came to court with their own infants, teens whose friends or family members had been killed by gang or domestic violence, kids who were physically or learning-disabled, and teens who were addicted.

I've seen attitudes and tears, denial and remorse. I've seen kids who asked to do jail time rather than pay a fine, parents who made their teens plead guilty on a misdemeanor just so they wouldn't have to come back to court, and people who fought a $20 seatbelt citation to the death. With the aid of a court interpreter, I've conducted hearings in Spanish, Russian, Armenian, Arabic, Hebrew, Farsi, Chinese, Korean, Japanese, and countless other languages.

Some stories broke my heart, but more than that, they taught me a lot about myself. One teen with multiple citations came to court with his mother. When I asked him where his dad was, he shrugged. Only after asking a lot of questions did I learn that he hadn't seen his father since he was two, and his mother's current husband was living on the streets. Another story involved a teen who had shoplifted from a department store. When I dug a little deeper into his history, I learned that the incident had occurred a month after he found his father dead from a suicide.

The case that changed me forever occurred a few months into my assignment to juvenile court. It involved a young man who had been involved in a school fight. He wore baggy clothes and his head looked shaved. I immediately assumed he was a gang member—just another one of the many I'd already seen. But he wasn't. His head wasn't shaven; he'd lost his hair while undergoing chemotherapy. His case—and many others—taught me to never make easy assumptions, to search deeper for answers and solutions that may not be readily apparent on the surface.

No matter who they were, what language they spoke, or what they were being charged with, all the teens who sat in my waiting room had one important thing in common: They were all asking themselves the same question—*What's going to happen to me?*

Some of the teens who appeared before me depended on friends for advice, but friends aren't always reliable sources of information because they aren't likely to understand the whole process. Some might even lie to preserve their own reputations. I once suspended a teen's license for street racing, imposing a hefty fine and ordering the teen to do community service. But after he walked out of the courtroom, the clerk overheard him telling his friends in the waiting room—who were about to have their own street-racing cases heard—that his ticket was dismissed.

So why did I want to pull back the curtain? First, because I've been inspired by the amazing people I have met during these past years: the sixty-year-old Japanese woman who adopted two teenage sisters whose parents were killed in the civil war in El Salvador; she barely spoke Spanish and the girls didn't speak Japanese or English, but somehow they made it work. And the father of a girl over whom two boys had fought; instead of getting mad at the boys, the father appeared in court to lend support to both of the young men. And the young woman who had been living in a foster home since she was twelve; her foster parents kicked her out the day she turned eighteen, but she held down two jobs and finished high school.

Also, more than just sharing the knowledge I've accumulated over the years, I wrote this guide because a citation to court is a chance to learn not only about the legal system, but about yourself, an opportunity to reflect on your future: Where are you now? Where do you want to be ten years from now? Waiting in court for your case to be heard is also a time to listen to other stories—to see and observe other people and their problems and behaviors, and to ask yourself, *Is this who I want to be? Do I want to be like them?* It's also a time to appreciate what you have instead of focusing on what you don't.

Lastly, there is one more reason. *Your* stories—the stories I have heard from the many teens I've seen over the years—have taught me that growing up is a lifetime experience. I've learned from you to appreciate my own life and children. Most of all, you've taught me how to stay young at heart and to try to avoid prejudgment.

In this guide you'll find information about the most common types of offenses committed by young people, help in deciphering your citation, and how to prepare for your court hearing. The guide will also give you tips designed to help you avoid getting future citations, myth busters, examples, stories, things to think about, and excerpts from actual letters and essays written to the court by teens like yourself about their personal experiences at juvenile court.

Disclaimer

This guide is meant to cover only a sampling of the infraction and lower-grade misdemeanor citations most often cited to minors. This guide does *not* cover misdemeanor and felony offenses for which a minor would normally be incarcerated or deemed a delinquent **ward** of the state, or cases in which a minor would become a **dependent child** of the state as a result of a finding of abuse and/or neglect.

This guide should not be considered formal legal advice, and nothing within this guide is intended to constitute a guarantee or prediction regarding the outcome of a juvenile matter. Every case is different, and outcomes will vary based on the unique facts and legal issues of each case.

Teen names included in this guide are completely fictional and are used only for the purpose of illustration.

CHAPTER 1

The Juvenile Court System

Who Is a Minor?

Before 1970 the **age of majority**—that is, the age at which a person legally becomes an adult—was twenty-one. In 1971 the Twenty-sixth Amendment to the U.S. Constitution was passed and most states changed the age of majority to eighteen. In most of the United States, a "juvenile" or "minor" is defined as someone who is under the age of eighteen, although in a few states the age of majority is higher—nineteen or twenty-one.

Before you reach the age of majority, you cannot enter into binding contracts; buy or sell property; marry without the consent of your parents; sue or be sued; settle a claim; inherit property outright; make or revoke a will; vote in national, state, or local elections; consent to medical treatment; or join the military without parental consent. There is also a separate court system for those who have not yet reached the age of majority.

The youngest age for juvenile court jurisdiction in delinquency matters is six years old, in North Carolina. Most states, however, have no specified minimum age in their state statutes or court rules. The oldest age for juvenile court jurisdiction in delinquency matters ranges from fifteen to seventeen. Many states also have an extended age over which a juvenile court may retain jurisdiction so that adults who were incarcerated as minors might still be separated from convicted adult populations.

The Philosophy and Purpose of the Juvenile Court

The purpose of the juvenile court is to provide for the safety and protection of both the public and the minor. The defined purposes of most state juvenile courts fall into one or more of five categories of legislation:

1. *Standard Juvenile Court Act* is modeled on an act originally issued in 1925 and subsequently revised many times: "Each child coming within the jurisdiction of the court shall receive . . . the care, guidance, and control that will conduce to his welfare and the best interest of the state."

2. *Balanced and Restorative Justice (BARJ)* advocates that juvenile courts give balanced attention to three primary interests: public safety, individual accountability to victims and the community, and the development in offenders of those skills necessary to live law-abiding and productive lives.

3. *Legislative Guide for Drafting Family and Juvenile Courts Acts*, published by the Children's Bureau in the late 1960s, which declares four purposes: (a) to provide for the care, protection, and mental development of children involved in the system; (b) to remove from children committing delinquent acts the consequences of criminal behavior and substitute a program of rehabilitation, supervision, and care; (c) to remove a child from the home when it is necessary; and (d) to assure all parties their constitutional and other legal rights.

4. *Additional clauses* that emphasize punishment, deterrence, accountability, and/or public safety. A small group of states emphasize community protection, offender accountability, crime reduction, and punishment as their predominant purposes.

5. *General "child welfare" laws* that emphasize the promotion of the best welfare and best interests of the juvenile as the sole or pri-

mary purpose of the juvenile court system. Incorporated by only a small number of states, these laws usually declare that the state will institute "all reasonable means and methods that can be established by a humane and enlightened state, solicitous of the welfare of its children, for the prevention of delinquency and for the care and rehabilitation of juvenile delinquents."

Why Is There a Separate System for Kids?

Even in the late eighteenth century, children as young as seven years old in the United States who broke the law could stand trial in criminal court for offenses and could be sentenced to prison or even given a death sentence. It was only in the nineteenth century that reformers lobbied for a change in the perception of children. These reformers maintained that children were persons who were not fully developed and needed specialized facilities that separated them from adult offenders. Juvenile courts were thereafter established in the first half of the twentieth century. Rather than punishing delinquents, these courts sought to treat youthful offenders and turn them into productive citizens.

In the 1960s and early 1970s the U.S. Supreme Court ruled on a series of landmark cases that dramatically changed the juvenile court justice system. In *Kent v. United States* (383 U.S. 541, 86 S. Ct. 1045 [1966]) the court decided that juveniles should be afforded the same constitutional rights as adults. In *In re Gault* (387 U.S. 1, 87 S. Ct. 1428 [1967]) the court ruled that in hearings that could result in commitment to an institution, juveniles had the right to notice and counsel, to question witnesses, and to protection against **self-incrimination**. In *In re Winship* (397 U.S. 358, 90 S.Ct. 1068 [1970]) the court found that the "**beyond a reasonable doubt**" standard applied to adults should also be applied in all delinquency adjudications. In *McKeiver v. Pennsylvania* (403 U.S. 528, 91 S.Ct. [1971]) the court confirmed that the due process clause of the Fourteenth Amendment did not require jury trials in juvenile proceedings.

In 1974 Congress passed the Juvenile Justice and Delinquency Prevention Act (JJDPA). Its primary goal was to protect juveniles by separating them from state court systems that were primarily meant to process adults. The law mandated that status offenders—those who commit crimes of status, meaning an offense that can only be committed by a minor and for which there is no adult equivalent, such as truancy or incorrigibility—would not be placed in secure correctional facilities. The law also required states to ensure that no juveniles be detained or confined in any adult jail or lockup. Additionally, the law prescribed that status offenders or juveniles found to be delinquent not have contact with adult inmates. Finally, the law defined the states' responsibility to address delinquency prevention and to reduce the disproportionate number of minority juveniles who come into contact with the justice system.

The 1974 act was a federal law, but in essence there are now fifty-one juvenile justice systems in the United States, and each state system has its own history, laws, and policies. State Criminal and Vehicle Code laws apply to minors just as they do to adults. However, each state has special codes that apply to minors and specific structures for handling juveniles. In California, for example, the Welfare and Institutions Code oversees the juvenile court system.

Types of Courts

There are many different names for the courts that handle juvenile cases. In Los Angeles, for example, the juvenile court system consists of a delinquency court, a dependency court, and an informal juvenile and traffic court. Traffic, pedestrian, status offenses, and many misdemeanors are funneled into the informal juvenile court through a notice to appear, or ticket, issued directly by a police officer. Other states, counties, or municipalities have various systems to deal with young people in court.

In Alabama criminal matters involving juveniles, called **informal adjustments**, are handled by a juvenile probation intake officer. In Alaska juvenile matters are handled by a juvenile probation intake officer who receives all delinquency referrals except for traffic and status offenses; the officer then makes diversion decisions. In Arkansas the circuit courts are in charge of juvenile matters; they use a graduated sanction system utilizing restorative services under the Department of Human Services, Division of Youth Services, Juvenile Justice Delinquency and Prevention Unit.

In New York the family court presides over juvenile matters. Cases may be taken directly to the court or with a notice to appear and a report to the county probation department. The case is then examined to see whether it should be referred for a formal **petition** to make a minor a delinquent ward of the court. An assistant corporation counsel presents the juvenile case on behalf of the state. In Colorado juvenile matters are handled by district court judges and magistrates. Connecticut has a Superior Court for Juvenile Matters.

Missouri and Oregon have youth courts; Ohio and New Mexico have established juvenile traffic courts; and Virginia has a juvenile and domestic relations court. Minnesota adjudicates minors under the age of nineteen at the Juvenile Family Justice Center. In Pennsylvania the Courts of Common Pleas exercise jurisdiction over delinquency matters. For a comprehensive look at each state's juvenile court system, go to the National Center for Juvenile Justice (NCJJ) Web site at www.ncjj.org/stateprofiles/ and select a state from the menu.

Some jurisdictions have established specialized juvenile drug courts to address drug-related offenses. Drug courts offer treatment and rehabilitation to substance abusers charged with nonviolent drug related offenses. Prosecution, supervision, or probation may be deferred pending successful participation in such a program. Minors receive treatment, health care, group and individual counseling, and educational and vocational training, and are tested for the use of controlled substances. Court supervision is more intense in these kinds of courts and may involve weekly or biweekly appearances before a judge.

Various forms of teen court, an early intervention alternative to the traditional justice system, have also cropped up all over the country. High school students who have been trained for this purpose act as bailiffs, court clerks, jury, and prosecution and defense attorneys. Although the proceedings are usually presided over by a real judge, these court hearings are considered nonjudicial diversion programs, and the juveniles being prosecuted must formally *agree* to be adjudicated and sentenced by a jury of their peers. The offenses adjudicated by this type of court encompass only infractions and less serious, low-grade misdemeanors

Finally, some jurisdictions refer all traffic and other infraction cases involving juveniles to adult court and do not have specialized courts or proceedings for these purposes.

Rehabilitation versus Punishment

I think everyone should get a second chance because you learn from your mistakes.

Historically, the purpose of juvenile court has been to rehabilitate rather than punish minors for illegal conduct. The system is rooted in the belief that young people are still in the process of maturing and cannot always fully appreciate the consequences of their actions. It's also based on the notion that young people can learn and change, and, given the proper level of accountability and programs, children and teens are still amenable to learning new behaviors.

For this reason, too, a special language is used with regard to minors to differentiate their hearings from adult proceedings. A trial, for example, is often called an **adjudication** or **contested hearing**. Minors are not convicted of crimes but are instead adjudicated wards of the state. Instead of sentencing hearings, dispositional hearings are conducted.

In the 1980s and 1990s, though, with juvenile crime on the increase, many people believed the juvenile system was too lenient and nearly every state passed more punitive juvenile laws that made it easier to try juveniles in adult court. Offenders charged with certain serious offenses were excluded from juvenile court jurisdiction, and **fitness hearings** were established to decide whether juveniles are "unfit" to be tried in juvenile court, and therefore transferred to adult court. Along with a minimum age requirement with regard to a finding that a minor is unfit to be tried in juvenile court, in making this determination the court will also take into consideration the minor's degree of criminal sophistication, whether the minor can be rehabilitated, the minor's previous delinquent history, and the success of previous attempts by the juvenile court to rehabilitate the minor.

Some jurisdictions, however, allow for the direct filing of serious juvenile cases in adult court without fitness hearings. Others use juvenile delinquency cases for future sentencing enhancements in adult cases. In 1994, California voters approved a ballot initiative called the "three strikes" law, which provides that people convicted of three serious felonies can face life in prison. Under that law, juvenile delinquency cases can be used as "strikes" (see California Penal Code, Section 667).

Although the trend toward more punitive solutions to teen crime continues, a new phenomenon that is gaining attention in some parts of the country is **therapeutic jurisprudence**, the use of the law as a therapeutic agent that targets and promotes alternative and constructive dispute resolution in family law, drug, and juvenile delinquency cases. Detractors, however, argue that this type of jurisprudence is a new strain of rehabilitationism and that certain human behaviors cannot be properly and effectively dealt with in court.

Confidentiality

Juvenile courts have been traditionally closed to the public. The commentary to the 1959 version of the Standard Juvenile Court Act, adopted by many states, designated hearings as "private," adding that reporters who attended juvenile court hearings should be permitted to do so with the understanding that they would not disclose the identity of the juvenile. This was based on the belief that youthful offenders should not be stigmatized forever because of their mistakes as minors. Another justification for confidentiality was to promote rehabilitation. The rationale was to prevent the humiliation and demoralization of publicity. Even now, cases involving juveniles do not publicly disclose family names. Minors are designated by their first name and first initial of their last name (such as "In the matter of Patrick T.").

High-profile crimes involving minors—such as the 1998 school yard shooting in Jonesboro, Arkansas—however, have led to changes in public attitudes about the juvenile justice system and youthful offenders' right to privacy. The rise in juvenile crime rates and the widespread media coverage of violent crimes committed by juveniles have driven many states to prosecute more juveniles as adults and to impose heavier sentences on juveniles.

Because the increase in violent crimes committed by juveniles has caused a shift away from goals of rehabilitation to those of punishment and deterrence, many states have opened juvenile proceedings to the public when a minor is charged with a violent crime. Court records and proceedings involving youths charged with offenses that would be considered felonies if committed by adults are public in Idaho, Indiana, Iowa, Maine, Maryland, Minnesota, Missouri, Utah, and Virginia. In Florida a law enforcement agency may release the name, picture, and address of a child charged with an offense that would constitute a felony if committed by an adult.

In California the public can be admitted to hearings when a juvenile is alleged to have committed a "felony criminal street gang activity," such as carjacking or drive-by shooting. In Illinois the public has the right of access to the name and address of any juvenile who is at least thirteen years old and has been criminally convicted of a serious crime or connected to criminal street gang activity. A Pennsylvania statute allows public access in felony cases when the defendant is over fourteen, and in specific serious felony cases—including murder, voluntary manslaughter, aggravated assault, arson, involuntary deviate sexual intercourse, kidnapping, rape, robbery, and carjacking—when the defendant is over twelve.

In 1997 an amendment to New York State's court rules created an explicit presumption that all family court proceedings, including juvenile proceedings, are open to the public, and members of the public have been admitted to several high-profile juvenile cases.

CHAPTER 2

I Received a Citation to Court

What Do I Do?

I don't know where to begin. If nothing else, just the fact that I knew what I was doing was wrong should have been more than enough to make me say no. The worst thing that could come out of this whole situation would be if I learned nothing, and shunned responsibility.

I always thought or assumed that I could get away with things due to the fact that I am a minor.

When I was pulled over my heart stopped. I hadn't even realized I was going 25 mph over the speed limit. The cop gave me a ticket and told me how at that speed there is no reaction time and if I hit anything I would disintegrate on impact.

The Stop

Being stopped or detained by a police officer is a scary and unsettling experience no matter who or how old you are. Even adults are often flustered or frustrated by a traffic enforcement stop or other type of police **detention**. Understanding the process, however, is helpful, whether you've already received a citation, also known as a ticket, or want to prevent the next one.

Law Enforcement—Who Are They, Exactly?

Uniformed law enforcement officers, or "cops," come from a variety of agencies. Most recognizable are city police officers, county sheriffs, and state highway patrol, but there are also park rangers, school police, housing police, parking violation officers, bus and subway/metro police officers, beach patrol, fish and game officers, ski patrol officers, and officers from dozens of other agencies. Each one is authorized under state or local laws and ordinances to cite for specific violations.

A law enforcement stop doesn't always immediately follow a violation. The police officer usually types in the license number of your vehicle in his mobile computer in order to gather as much information as possible before he detains you. For officer safety purposes, he wants to know whether he's dealing with a typical citizen stop or if the vehicle has been reported stolen. This information will dictate the manner in which he approaches your vehicle. It may take a few minutes for the information to come up on his computer, so don't be surprised if he follows your vehicle for a few blocks until he's certain as to how to proceed.

If you're signaled by a police officer to pull over, you should

1. slow down,
2. turn on your blinker, and
3. stop at the side of the road as soon as it is safe to do so.

You want to indicate your intention to cooperate with the officer as soon as possible.

Once you've properly stopped the car, don't get out of the car unless you're instructed to do so. You should roll down your window and put both your hands on the wheel. Don't reach over into your glove compartment until you're asked to do so. Any sudden moves can be interpreted as reaching for a weapon. Stay calm and cooperative and answer all pertinent questions. Getting agitated or confrontational with the officer will only escalate an already difficult situation.

Tip

If you're stopped by a police officer, always keep your hands visible. In a car, don't remove your seatbelt unless you are asked to do so. On the street, keep your hands in view of the officer and don't reach into pockets.

The same applies if you're approached on the street. Stop immediately and don't attempt to run away. Listen carefully and obey all the officer's directives.

Sean D. and five friends decided to skateboard at a closed school campus on New Year's Day. A neighbor reported trespassers to the police, who came to investigate. When an officer called the subjects over to the fence, four of the skateboarders complied, but two ran away and hid on campus. The four compliant subjects were merely **counseled and released**, meaning they were verbally warned about their offenses but did not receive citations. Sean was one of the skateboarders who ran away. He was cited for trespassing, something he could have avoided if he had not run away from police.

Manuel D.'s investigation report described a detention stop that ended badly. On routine patrol, an officer saw Manuel standing behind a large electrical box that appeared to have been vandalized. Suspicious of criminal activity, the officer exited his patrol vehicle and ordered Manuel to stop. Instead, Manuel began walking away. The officer continued to command Manuel to stop, but Manuel ignored his commands. The officer also noticed that his hands were concealed in the front of his waistband. The officer ordered him to stop and show his hands. Manuel continued to disobey the officer's orders. Eventually Manuel was overtaken by the officer and pepper-sprayed when he resisted. Manuel was charged with vandalism and disobeying the orders of a police officer.

When you are stopped, the officer should identify himself and his agency to you. If you don't understand who has stopped and cited you, don't be afraid to ask which agency the officer represents. At the stop, be honest about your name, age, phone number, and home address. Any false information you relate to an officer will eventually be discovered and will make your situation worse. The officer will probably cross-check information you've given him by calling your school and your parents, or using his police vehicle computer.

Amanda T. was stopped with a group of her friends at a mall while they were ditching school. She gave her own name along with her sister's date of birth and a cousin's address. Amanda was later charged with **giving false information to an officer**; the additional charge was more serious than the truancy for which she was originally detained.

Tip

Don't struggle with police or resist arrest. If you're injured in an arrest, take photographs immediately. You can respectfully decline permission for the police to search you. However, limited pat-down searches to check for weapons are permitted for an officer's protection, and no consent is required. If you're arrested, it's best to remain silent. Be careful what you say to your parents when they arrive at the police station; you have no right to privacy in a police station.

I was dropped off at school, but I then met up with my friends and started walking across the street. We got into another friend's car. I was planning on trying marijuana for the first time. Once people started smoking I was waiting for my turn when the officers stopped us. The officer asked me for my phone number and parents' names, and I was so scared I gave them fake names and phone numbers. That was a big mistake. I will never give false information again.

Probable Cause

An officer must have **probable cause** in order to stop you and give you a ticket or citation. This means that an officer cannot stop or detain you unless he has a specific reason or cause to do so. Equipment or registration violations, for example, are considered probable cause to stop you.

A court will determine whether probable cause existed for purposes of arrest by examining the facts and circumstances within the officer's knowledge to discover whether they are sufficient to cause a prudent person to believe a suspect has committed, is committing, or is about to commit a crime. (If you're interested in reading the Supreme Court case, see *U.S. v. Puerta*, 982 F.2d 1297, 1300 [9th Cir. 1992].)

With regard to seizure of items, probable cause merely requires that the facts available to the officer warrant a person of "reasonable caution" to conclude that certain items may be contraband or stolen property or useful as evidence of a crime. (See *U.S. v. Dunn*, 946 F.2d 615, 619 [9th Cir. 1991], cert. Denied, 112 S. Ct. 401 [1992].)

Miranda Advisements

A typical ticket or citation stop is considered a "detention" and is not an "arrest," for which the officer would be obligated to inform you of your **Miranda rights**. Miranda rights stem from the landmark 1966 Supreme Court case *Miranda v. Arizona* [384 U.S. 436 (1966)], in which the Supreme Court ruled that anyone taken into police custody for questioning must be first advised of his or her constitutional rights, including the right to remain silent, the right to speak with a lawyer, and the right to have a lawyer present during questioning.

Although you will not be advised of your Miranda rights at a standard traffic stop, you should be advised of these rights if you are questioned in the field, at a police station, or by school police.

Other Advisements and Determinations

In California and in other jurisdictions, minors under the age of fourteen who are cited at school are questioned under the guidelines of a case called *In re Gladys R*(1 Cal. 3d 855 [1970]). The case

A reading of Miranda rights typically contains the following oral advisements:

1. You have the right to remain silent and refuse to answer questions. Do you understand?
2. Anything you do say may be used against you in a court of law. Do you understand?
3. You have the right to consult an attorney before speaking to the police and to have an attorney present during questioning now or in the future. Do you understand?
4. If you cannot afford an attorney, one will be appointed for you before any questioning if you wish. Do you understand?
5. If you decide to answer questions now without an attorney present you will still have the right to stop answering at any time until you talk to an attorney. Do you understand?
6. Knowing and understanding your rights as I have explained them to you, are you willing to answer my questions without an attorney present?

provides that a determination must be made as to whether a minor understands the wrongfulness of his or her behavior, and whether he or she knows the meaning of the words "lawyer," "judge," "court," "right to remain silent," "appointed," and so on.

In Los Angeles, for example, school police officers fill out a two-page questionnaire with inquiries such as: "Do you know the difference between doing what's right and doing what's wrong?" "Give me an example of something right to do." "Give me an example of something wrong to do." The questionnaire directs the officer to ask questions in simple words. For example, he would use the phrase "take something that doesn't belong to you" instead of **petty theft**; "go into a house without permission to take something that isn't yours" instead of **burglary**; or "start a fight or hit someone" instead of **assault** or **battery**.

Resisting or Not Following Orders of a Police Officer

When an officer asks you to stop on the street or flashes police lights behind you, if you are in a car, you are obligated to stop and answer questions. Fleeing the scene, resisting arrest, or not following the orders of a police officer will only serve to worsen the situation and subject you to charges for additional offenses.

Edmond D. jumped over the school fence and was placed under arrest for truancy by his school police. He was taken to the school office but refused to answer questions or cooperate in any way. He then threatened to spit on the officer, pushed the door to the office with his head, and yelled obscenities. His actions escalated the situation from an unsecured detention to a secured detention, where he was placed in wrist locks.

Detention and Arrest

In some more serious instances, you might be detained by police for questioning. A detention is not an arrest, but may lead to one. You might be detained at the scene of the offense or incident, or be transported in a police car to a police station for further investigation. You could be handcuffed and pat-down searched if circumstances warrant.

At the police station, you might be placed in a **juvenile holding tank.** At that point you would be advised of your right to make a telephone call to your parents or attorney. Depending on the circumstances, you may be released to your parents.

The Citation

What Does Signing My Citation Mean?

This year has been my year of painful learning. I had to learn what it took to be part of a championship football team, and how hard it actually was to work and support myself, but something else taught me a big lesson: getting a ticket.

When a police officer asks you to sign your citation, also called a **notice to appear**, he's asking you to sign a *promise* to appear in court instead of being detained at the police station. You're not admitting guilt by signing the citation; you're only promising to appear in court rather than being arrested on the spot. If you refuse to sign the ticket, the officer will be forced to take you into custody, that is, transport you to the police station and book you.

Tip

Try not to lose your copy of the ticket. Although most times you'll be able to track down a citation, court dates, and court locations, this may not always be an easy process.

Typically, what you are signing will read something like this:

> Without admitting guilt, I promise to appear at the time and place indicated below.

After the officer writes up the citation, and you sign it, the officer should give you a copy for your records.

Tell Your Parents

> *Starting today I'm going to be honest with my mom with everything. I know it was wrong of me not telling her what happened, but I was afraid how she would react to it.*

The officer might call your parents or accompany you home. If he allows you to go home by yourself, tell your parents immediately. Don't wait weeks or even days to tell them. The sooner you get it over with, the better. Remember, your parents may have to ask for time off from their jobs in advance in order to accompany you to court.

If your parents are divorced or separated, make sure you inform both. Jamie T.'s divorced parents had joint custody of Jamie.

Although Jamie told his mother about his first speeding ticket, he neglected to mention it to his dad. At Jamie's hearing on the second ticket, Jamie's father felt embarrassed when the judge informed him of Jamie's other ticket. As a result, Jamie's father immediately cancelled Jamie's car insurance and took away his car.

Understanding the Citation

My parents always told me to be careful, but my parents can only tell me so many times. At the end of the day, it's up to me.

I know that I messed up badly. If I would just do the things I'm supposed to do, nothing would be so complicated.

The citation should always include the date and time the offense occurred; the place where it occurred; the code section or statute you were cited under; information about your vehicle (if a vehicle was involved) such as registration, VIN number, year of the vehicle, and make and model; your driver's license number; your address and phone number; your gender, height, weight, age, birth date, race, hair, and eye color; and sometimes a short narration or diagram. Some newer forms also include a space for your thumbprint.

Tip

Your parents won't be happy to find a ticket crumpled up on the desk in your room or at the bottom of your pants pocket. They don't want to be surprised by a letter in the mail from the court or the DMV. You should be the one to tell your parents about your ticket.

The citation should also list the name of the officer, her station and badge number, and any possible future vacation dates where she will be unable to testify, should she receive a **subpoena** to appear in court. This information is important to you, especially if you have any questions. Virginia M. was offended by the officer's conduct when she was stopped for a red light. "He brought me to tears," she said in court. I told her that if there was anything unprofessional about the officer's conduct at the time she was cited, she could easily track down the officer's station and supervisor by using the information on her citation.

As previously mentioned, there are a number of agencies that cite minors in your city—police, sheriff's department, park rangers, highway patrol, school police, and so on. Each of their tickets may look a little different, but all should contain the same relevant information.

The officer should sign and correctly date the citation. The arresting or citing officer will usually state the following if she has personally witnessed the offense:

> I declare under penalty of perjury under the laws of the state of _____, the foregoing is true and correct.

Abbreviations used on your ticket may include:

Btwn.: Between
DL: Driver's License
Est.: Estimated
Ins.: Insurance
Lft.: Left
N/B: Northbound
OBSD: Observed
Pass.: Passenger
P/C: Probable Cause
Ped.: Pedestrian
Pkd.: Parked
Poss.: Possession
RD: Reporting District
Reg.: Registration
Req.: Required
R/P: Reporting Party
Rt.: Right
S/B: Southbound
Spd.: Speed
Subj.: Subject
W/O: Without

Additionally, you might also see numbers on the citation that indicate the specific number of a radar or laser unit.

If the arresting officer has not personally witnessed the violation—for example, if she's received a radio call about a shoplifting and the store witnesses have made statements leading her to believe a shoplifting has occurred—she will check off the following statement:

> Violations not committed in my presence, declared on information and belief.

What Is an Infraction and What Is a Misdemeanor?

If you receive a citation or notice to appear in court, you have most likely been charged with an infraction or a misdemeanor.

An **infraction** is a violation *not* punishable by imprisonment, such as most traffic offenses, for example, failure to stop at a stop sign or red light.

A **misdemeanor** is an offense for which the punishment is a fine and/or up to one year in a county jail. Misdemeanor offenses include petty theft, a first-time **DUI** (driving under the influence of alcohol or drugs), and **hit-and-run**.

A **felony** is the most serious type of crime and is punishable by a fine and/or imprisonment of more than one year. Some felonies are punishable by a death sentence. A felony is *not* a **citable offense**, that is, an offense for which you would receive a notice to appear in court at some later date. A felony is an offense for which you would be arrested and immediately arraigned in court.

What Am I Cited For?

Don't rely on what you think the officer said to you at the time of the citation. You may have misunderstood or been too nervous to understand clearly. Also, although officers are trained to interact with the public, they aren't always good at relaying this information. Officers sometimes try to neutralize tension by saying, "You'll probably get a warning in court" or "You can just go to traffic school and get this off your record." This is not necessarily so. If the officer had wanted to give you a "warning," no citation would have been issued.

Finally, the officer doesn't have the final say-so about traffic school or any other type of disposition—that's up to the judge.

It's always a good idea to understand your citation by looking up the **code section** in your local public library, county law library, or on the Internet. The code will not be written out in its entirety, but in abbreviated form (for example, P.C. for Penal Code, V.C. for Vehicle Code, H&S for Health and Safety Code). Make sure you are looking at the latest version of that law, as laws are often amended, or revised, from year to year.

Tip

Read your citation carefully. What's most relevant to the court is what's written on the citation, not what the officer said or didn't say to you at the time of the violation.

Aidan B. looked up the code section for his red light violation. After reading the code section, he realized that the officer had cited him for the wrong subsection of the law. Subsection (a) of the code provided that a driver should stop completely at a red light. However, Adrian had violated subsection (b), making a right turn on a red light without stopping. This mistake gave Adrian a good defense to his ticket.

Alteration

The citation should not be altered or marked up in any way. You have only one of many copies of the citation generated by the police officer. Law enforcement and the court will retain the other copies, including the original. If you alter your copy, the court will know, and could possibly add an extra offense to your citation.

Gina B. was so afraid to show her speeding ticket to her parents that she altered her ticket to show 70 mph instead of 90 mph. The judge showed her parents the original citation. She was given an additional fine and suspension time for altering the citation, along with the punishments she received at home.

Mistakes on the Citation

A citation is a legal document and is like a **pleading** presented to a court. It should be accurate, and it must be signed and dated by both the officer and the person receiving the citation. Judges understand, however, that citations are written "in the field," sometimes in the rain or other difficult roadside conditions. An officer may also write several citations at one time, such as multiple stops, where the officer is citing a group of people.

Few written mistakes are "fatal" to a citation, meaning they warrant an immediate dismissal. Most hastily written errors on a citation are considered ***de minimus*** (Latin, for "not important" or "minor"). Remember too that the officer can send you an **amendment** to the citation by mail. Amendments are usually accepted up to the time of a trial.

The nature and relevance of the officer's error is also taken into consideration. The time your ticket was written is normally *not* important to a speeding ticket. But an incorrect time can be crucial if the ticket is for a violation for making a left turn at an intersection that allows no left turns between 4 and 7 p.m.

In citations where the code section doesn't match the narrative, this discrepancy could be considered a **fatal flaw**, a mistake that is grounds for dismissal. For example, if the code section relates to a stop sign, but the narrative describes a red light violation, this is a fatal flaw.

If the ticket doesn't warrant an instant dismissal on arraignment, you still have an opportunity to raise these **credibility** issues at a trial. You can argue that the officer's mistakes on the ticket give rise to questions as to whether he was really paying attention at the time of the offense—and if so, could he also have been mistaken about the offense itself?

Adrian D.'s ticket was written on January 3, 2005, but the officer mistakenly wrote 2004 on the ticket. Adrian contended at court that his ticket should be dismissed based on this mistake. I ruled that the error was not serious, but rather a natural mistake, due to the fact that it had only been a couple of days after the first of the year. Had the officer written the wrong year three months later, I probably would have ruled differently.

MYTH: Mistakes on my citation will get my ticket dismissed.

MYTH BUSTER: A couple of insignificant mistakes on your citation are not automatically cause to dismiss your ticket. A good rule of thumb is that a minor mistake or two does not warrant a dismissal, but a lot of mistakes might. If, for example, on a speeding ticket the officer checks off that you're a male (when you're a female), neglects to enter the speed your car was traveling, and enters the wrong date, this would probably add up to a dismissal.

Other Reports

Police Reports

Typically, you will only be handed a citation at a stop. In some cases, however, a police report may be generated at a later date. If a police report has been written and filed, you have the right to a copy of the police report or officer's notes made in connection to your citation. A request for this report is called a **discovery request**, which is a pretrial procedure compelling the disclosure of pertinent factual information.

The report usually includes a narrative as to the circumstances of the stop; the names, phone numbers, addresses and statements of witnesses; and any observations or conclusions the officer may have made as a result of an investigation. A typical report may read like this:

> On 04/06/07 at approximately 0820 hours, I, Officer Smith, #1208, was working for the Los Angeles Police Department

> in full uniform and marked police vehicle assigned to juvenile enforcement. While patrolling the area, I observed two juveniles at Doe Park with their backpacks loitering during school hours. As soon as the juveniles saw my patrol vehicle, one of the juveniles grabbed something from the bench and quickly placed the item inside his pant pocket as if he was trying to hide the item. Upon contact with the juveniles, they appeared extremely nervous. Subject #1 became very pale. I asked them if they were carrying anything they weren't supposed to be carrying and Subject #1 answered "maybe." I then conducted a consensual search of both subjects and felt a large bulge on Subject #1's pants pocket. Subject #1 stated that the bulge was a pipe. I then removed the glass pipe which contained burned residue resembling marijuana.

Witness Reports and Statements

A witness report describes in as much detail as possible the nature of the incident, who was involved, and the date, time, and location of the incident. The following is an example of a school witness statement:

> I noticed a boy and a girl (former student) talking to each other outside my classroom backdoor. Initially, I wasn't paying a lot of attention except that they were acting very odd. So I watched more carefully and saw the children take each other's hands as if passing something. I immediately ran out my other door to catch them before they got away. The boy tried to walk off. Luckily an adult came up who knew the boy and he stopped. I asked to see what was in their hands. The girl hesitated and finally showed me a small bag of weed. I called the dean's office.

Traffic Collision Reports

If your citation was a result of an accident, a traffic collision report might be attached. It would contain information as to the primary collision factor, including the party most at fault, weather conditions, lighting, roadway surface and conditions, traffic control devices, any drug or other physical factors or obstructions, and other associated factors.

For example, in a collision involving a fire hydrant, the investigating police officer wrote a narrative that explained what happened to Arden G., who was cited for making an unsafe left turn:

> P/1 [party 1] said he was traveling E/B [eastbound] on Main approaching Elm. He conducted a left turn onto Main and while conducting this turn he lost control of his vehicle, causing him to exit the roadway and collide into a fire hydrant. His vehicle came to rest on top of the fire hydrant which was spouting high pressured water. P/1 attempted to move his vehicle from the fire hydrant, but was unable to do so.

CHAPTER 3

Preparing for Court

The worst part of all this was having to start all over with regaining the trust of my parents and trying to start the process of increasing my freedom after it had just begun to open up for me.

You have ample time between the date of your citation and your court date to prepare for your court case. It's a good idea to use this time to find out as much information as possible. In certain jurisdictions, you may be able to look up your citation, check its status, request traffic school, request extensions, and so on, online. In some states, however—California, for example—tickets cited to juveniles are confidential and cannot be accessed online. The time between the date of your citation and your court date is also a good time to gather up documents that may be helpful to your case.

Understanding Court Dates and Times

The process that I have gone through, including the initial court appearance, has come together to impact my life and my thinking.

The usual time frame for citing into court is anywhere from thirty to sixty days after your citation. Some courts allow you to come *on or before*, but this also depends on whether your ticket has been entered into the court's computer system. Check with your local court. "On or before" might mean three weeks before, but it might also mean only three days before. Remember that tickets are generated not by the court, but by law enforcement agencies who are separate entities from the court. Allow a reasonable time for law enforcement to process and send their tickets to the court.

Aaron F. received a ticket for running a red light. Two days later he appeared in court for his ticket. Unfortunately, his ticket wouldn't arrive in court for another six weeks. He requested a dismissal of his ticket, based on the fact that he had appeared and the ticket was not heard by the judge. He learned that he could not expect a dismissal of his ticket just because he appeared in court far ahead of his court date, and the ticket was not as yet in the system.

What If I'm Going to Be Away on My Court Date? Are There Grace Periods?

Some jurisdictions allow a **continuance** (also known as an **extension**)—a postponement of the original court date on your citation—to be requested by phone or mail; others require that requests be made in person. Check with the court to which you've been cited to appear. If there's a legitimate reason that you or your parent cannot appear on your court date, call or write the court. Legitimate reasons might include being out of town or out of the country, school testing, medical problems, or being away at boarding school. If you call, always record the time and date of the call as well as the name of the person you spoke with. Also be aware that some violations are not eligible for an extension.

Helen N. called the court about not being able to appear for her court date. She thought she had been given a verbal continuance, only to realize three weeks later—and after she received a letter from the Department of Motor Vehicles—that she had contacted the wrong court.

It's better to write a letter and explain your particular circumstances. Every letter addressed to the court will be logged in and attached to your case file. Although some courts use e-mail for internal purposes, they may not use e-mail for correspondence with the public.

Tip

If you're sending a letter to the court, mail it with a signature or delivery confirmation. Written proof of mailing is better evidence than your unverifiable statement that you attempted to contact the court.

Failure to Appear

If you don't appear on your court date, the court may issue a warrant and notify the DMV to suspend your driving privileges, or it may charge only a **failure to appear** but still notify the DMV to suspend your driving privileges. The court may notify the DMV as to other infractions and misdemeanors as well as driving infractions. If you show up days or weeks late to court, you will face additional consequences. A failure to appear offense will be added to your original citation and may result in additional fines.

If you didn't inform the court by calling or writing, at the very least bring proof of your alleged justifiable reason for your failure to appear. This could be a medical problem or condition (in that case, bring a letter—on letterhead—from a doctor or hospital) or being out of the country (bring your passport) or state (bring airline tickets).

Many courts will issue a **bench warrant**, meaning a warrant issued by the judge, for your arrest if you don't show up for court. Warrants are very expensive and a **recall of warrant** can only be issued by the court. They may also land you in juvenile hall.

Running Away from Home

I'm here because I missed court and ran away from home. So therefore, I am messing up. Even as a fourteen-year-old the decisions I make today can have a long-lasting effect on my future. And if that is the concept you think I am not grasping and understanding, I obviously am, if I can explain it.

> **Something to Think About**
>
> Imagine how awful it would be for your parents to have to file a missing persons report on you, a report that typically includes the name and address of your dentist, because dental records are sometimes the only way to identify the remains of some missing persons.

Running away from home isn't itself a crime, but running away from your court date is. Unfortunately, some teens not only fail to tell their parents about their citations and/or fail to appear in court, but actually run away from home, staying with friends—or worse, on the streets. Running away very often leads to you being victimized.

> **Tip**
>
> Citations, just like any other problems, catch up with you no matter what. Facing your problems at the outset is a lot easier than facing them later.

Trial by Declaration

Some courts will allow you to request a trial by declaration. This is a procedure where, instead of going to court for a trial on your citation, you mail or bring in a written statement on a special form explaining the facts of your case and why the court should rule in your favor. You should also include any documentary evidence you feel might be helpful. In a trial by declaration, you waive your rights to appear, to testify in person, and to subpoena witnesses. In some jurisdictions trial by declaration is not available to minors.

Pre-Hearing Contract

In certain cases, the district attorney or a DA hearing officer may evaluate a case before filing it in court and recommend a contract between the district attorney's office and the minor *instead* of a court hearing.

In a pre-hearing contract, the minor admits his actions were improper and accepts responsibility. The minor and his parents then consent to participate in the agreement with the understanding that if the minor fails to live up to the agreement, a petition may be filed against him.

The case is monitored by the district attorney for a certain period of time (usually one year) and may include an agreement to maintain good grades and attendance, and participate in counseling, community service, drug and alcohol treatment, and parenting classes.

What Should I Bring to Court?

Documents

Give some thought as to which **mitigating factors** or explanatory documents might be helpful to your case. If you've committed a hit-and-run, for example, but your insurance company (or you personally) compensated the victim, bring documents to show that you tried to make the victim whole, meaning that you have tried to "right the wrong" committed against the victim. Sometimes the disposition of your case will rest on whether you've tried to make amends.

Janet Z. drove without a license and then had an accident with a parked vehicle. She pleaded guilty to the offense of driving without a license but contested the charge of hit-and-run. Janet brought proof to court that she had entered into an agreement with the victim's insurance company to pay off the expenses related to the accident. The allegation of hit-and-run was reduced to a **lesser charge**, meaning a less serious offense.

> **Tip**
>
> The time between your citation and your court date is your *window of opportunity*, a time you can use to present positive behavior, good citizenship, and character references that may lessen the severity of your disposition.

Helen P. committed a shoplifting offense. When she appeared in court, she presented me with the apology letter she wrote and sent to the shop owner, along with proof that she had paid the storeowner for the item she stole. Her proactive conduct prior to the court hearing helped in reducing the offense to a lesser charge.

School Records

How you do in school speaks volumes about who you are. But it's not only about good grades; attendance is also important. Do you go to school every day, or do you ditch or cut classes? Are you often tardy for first period or other classes? Do you have unexcused absences? If you're failing a class, it's helpful to show the judge you've signed up for summer school or intersession to make it up; this is a show of **good faith**, meaning you've been trying to make up for your offense even before you're ordered to do so by the court.

> **Tip**
>
> Be proactive. If the grades on your last report card are poor but you've recently improved, circulate a weekly progress and attendance report to your teachers that you can present to the judge. If you're failing a class, ask your teacher what you can do to pass—maybe do an extra credit report or take a make-up exam.

If you're in special education or undergoing an individualized education program (IEP), bring proof of this to court.

Character References

Letters from teachers, employers, coaches, or clergy can help in the disposition of your case. Don't be embarrassed about asking for them. I've found that people who care about you will be happy to write you a letter to present to the court. These kinds of letters won't serve to dismiss your case, but they may be helpful in easing the harshness of your sentence.

Remember, though, to present your documents in a professional manner. Torn-off, handwritten letters from a school notebook won't make a good impression, and they might not even be acceptable. Stationery or letterhead makes a better presentation and better evidence in court.

College Acceptance, Military Papers, or Job Corps

If you've been accepted to college or joined the military, present your college acceptance letter or ship-out letters to the court. These are positive indications of your character, abilities, and aspirations. You can also ask your military recruiter to accompany you to court. Recruiters are very often happy to do this, as all citations need to be resolved before you can ship out.

If you've joined Job Corps—a nationwide residential and educational training program for economically challenged youth ages sixteen through twenty-four that provides academic, vocational, and life skills training as well as a GED program—bring your acceptance letter.

Drug Tests

If you have a drug-related case, you should prove to the judge that you're drug free at the time of your hearing. A clean drug test will help bolster your argument that your drug incident wasn't habitual. The judge will view the time between the citation and the court date as time you could have used to make changes in your life. If, on the other hand, you're still using drugs or alcohol, the judge will view this as a missed opportunity on your part, as well as a further exercise of bad judgment or proof that your drug problem is long-term.

Bring documentation of a drug test result from a legitimate lab, your doctor, or a known drug rehabilitation facility. Home drug tests are not always reliable and are not acceptable in court.

Alan D.'s family went one step further. After he was caught at school with drugs, his favorite uncle made him a five-by-five-foot sign that read: "I am a moron. I got caught with drugs at school."

For the next two days Alan stood on a street corner with his sign and a flag, waving to the passersby. When he came to court, he brought the written journal of his two days on the street corner and a photo of himself with the sign.

> Nonstop I had to wave the flag. A lot of people stopped to talk to me that day. They told me their stories about drug problems, what happened to them and their family members.

Alan's punishment was extreme and not at all typical, but informing the court about any punishments, grounding, loss of privileges, home service, loss of allowance, loss of car, and so on will give the judge a better idea of how your family deals with behavioral issues. Although punishments at home are not a substitute for a court disposition, they might be taken into consideration in terms of the severity of orders. Clearly, a family unit that takes an offense seriously may need less court intervention and/or supervision.

Proof of Employment

If you're employed, you might want to bring with you proof of employment to show that you're responsible, paying your own way, or contributing to your family's budget. Also, if you're doing any volunteer work on your own accord—not because it's required at your school—bring along proof of your volunteering activities.

Letters from Therapists

If you're going to therapy, a rehabilitation facility, or a twelve-step program such as Alcoholics Anonymous, Marijuana Anonymous, or Narcotics Anonymous, don't just tell the judge—prove it to him or her in writing. If your **sponsor** is willing, have him or her accompany you to court.

In most cases, your therapist does not have to write a detailed case history. A short letter explaining that you are actively working on your problems or issues, are attending regular appointments, and are motivated will suffice. It tells the judge you're trying to turn things around.

If you've been diagnosed with depression, have been hospitalized, have ADHD, are bipolar, or have any other psychological condition, it's a good idea to bring documentation of your condition to court. Let the judge know whether you're taking a prescribed medication for your condition.

Tip

Don't be embarrassed to discuss or bring to court proof of *extenuating*, meaning explanatory, issues or circumstances. The more information the judge has, the better your outcome will be.

Letters to the Judge

Dear Judge: I hope that I have made it abundantly clear that I have taken and continue to take steps toward positive societal contribution. I hope we can work out a mutually satisfactory solution.

A juvenile court judge will certainly welcome any letters written by you prior to your court appearance. You may send the letter before your court hearing, hand the letter to the judge at the hearing, or even ask permission to read it out loud in court. Writing a letter shows you've given your offense some thought and have taken the time to communicate your feelings about your conduct on paper.

Tip

A letter you write for the judge can be helpful in sorting out your own feelings as much as showing your remorse to the judge.

Most teens have difficulty expressing themselves under the stress of a court appearance. Writing a letter will give you the opportunity to express yourself clearly without pressure. It might also help you clarify to yourself why you committed your offense.

Letter to a Victim

If there's a victim involved in a case, you might want to write a letter of apology to her and give the judge a copy. Here's an example of a letter written by a teen to the manager of a store:

> I'm very sorry that I would even think about stealing something from your store, yet I did. This note is to apologize for what I took and to state that I will never steal again. I'm extremely embarrassed for putting you in that position and taking up your time, which I know is very valuable. I know I disrespected you. My actions were stupid, wrong, inconsiderate and disrespectful. Your store is one of my favorites and I'm very sorry.

Driver's Licenses and Other Permits or Certificates

Make sure you bring your license, permit, or training certificates to court, especially if you are appearing for a driving, alcohol/drug, or vandalism offense. You may be tempted to leave your license at home or claim that you've lost it or it was stolen because you're afraid of or expecting a possible suspension. Know, however, that a court can suspend your license without actually taking possession of it, and most courts have immediate access to DMV and law enforcement databases. If you claim your license has been lost or stolen, the court will probably require you to bring a duplicate from the Department of Motor Vehicles.

Jennifer C. came to court on a speeding ticket. When asked to present her license, she claimed she'd lost it. But when the court told her she'd have to go to DMV to get a duplicate one—and her mom realized they'd have to spend an entire day standing in line at the DMV to obtain the duplicate—her license was miraculously found twenty minutes later. Her less-than-forthright behavior affected her credibility at her hearing.

Proof of Correction or "Fix-it" Tickets

The exhaust I added to my dad's car was a very childish decision. I did it to show off and impress my friends, but it wasn't worth it. I soon learned it was an attention grabber, attracting police attention, along with being a public annoyance.

If you have a ticket that's a **correctable violation**, you may be able to substantially lower your fine by correcting the offense. The ticket itself will indicate whether or not your violation is correctable. These types of offenses usually include expired registration, proof of insurance, tinted windows, or an equipment violation such as a broken taillight or a noisy modified muffler. In California, for example, if you are given a **fix-it ticket** by a police officer, the "yes" box will be checked next to "Correctable Violation," and after the problem is fixed, you must get the signature of an authorized person (i.e., a local law enforcement officer) on the **certificate of correction** portion of the ticket. If you are issued a fix-it ticket for an unlawful vehicle modification in your state, read the ticket to determine whether you can mail in the proof of correction or if you are still required to appear personally in court. Receipts from an auto supply store will not usually suffice to dismiss a correctable violation citation.

Some courthouses have inspection areas nearby for your convenience, but others may not, so make a phone call ahead of time. Proof of correction may save you money and result in a dismissal of your ticket. If you're driving a car that doesn't belong to you, it doesn't necessarily mean you're off the hook for correctable violations. The ticket doesn't always go to the registered owner; as the driver, you're responsible for whatever car you're driving.

Think about the consequences of any modifications you make to your own car. For example, many teens like the sleek, dark look of tinted windows. They look cool, right? But if your windows are tinted too dark, this will give an officer a good reason to stop you. This holds true for mufflers that are altered to sound louder, illegal blue lights, and so on. Do you really want to spend time and money on all sorts of add-ons, only to have to remove them?

Sometimes exceptions are made for people who have a medical reason for making a modification that would otherwise be illegal. If you have a medical condition that directly relates to your violation, for example a sensitivity to light that requires you to tint your car windows, this might qualify you for an exemption to the offense of illegal tinted windows. Bring proper documentation of this condition to court.

> **Tip**
>
> If you're driving an unfamiliar car that belongs to a friend or family member, make sure to determine beforehand whether the car is insured and the registration fees have been paid, and test out the brakes, turn signals, lights, and tires before driving.

Adam W. presented such a note at his hearing for a violation regarding tinted windows. The problem with the note, however, was that the patient indicated was Adam's father, not Adam. He was not the person listed, so Adam didn't qualify for the exception. The reasoning is similar to the one used with regard to handicap parking tags: If the handicap parking tag is assigned to your mother or grandmother and the person to whom it is assigned is not with you in the car, you've committed an offense.

Receipts and Letters from a Mechanic

A receipt from an auto parts store or mechanic may be helpful to show that there was something wrong with your car—brakes, transmission, and so on. Keep in mind, however, that many privately owned mechanic shops may not be able to write you a letter descriptive enough for the court, but the service department of an authorized auto dealership might. The receipt should be dated to correlate the repair with your citation.

Proof the Car Has Been Sold, Totaled, or Stolen

If your car has been sold and you no longer have possession in order to "fix" the offense, bring proof that you've sold the car and it is no longer owned by you. Proof might be shown by a **release of liability** form issued by your local DMV. By the same token, if your car has been in an accident and totaled or is still at the mechanic's, bring proof of that to court. If your car has been stolen, bring a police report proving the date of the theft.

> **Tip**
>
> Driving without a license is not usually considered correctable, but if you've been cited for that offense, try to obtain a license or permit in the interim. If you're in the process of obtaining your license and are currently enrolled in driver's education, you might ask the court for some extra time to procure the license. Note that some courts may allow you time, others may not, and times will vary from court to court—but it doesn't hurt to make the request.

Speedometer Calibrations

If you have a speeding violation and you're contesting it, be proactive and have your speedometer calibrated. **Calibration** is *not* something that normally occurs at your regular oil change or tune-up; you have to specifically request it and it requires special calibration machinery. A calibration determines whether the speed shown on your speedometer is accurate. Remember, the officer will usually bring proof of his patrol car's speedometer calibration or proof of radar or laser calibration. If you say, "I think my speedometer works fine," that will hold no weight against an officer's documentary evidence.

> **Tip**
>
> Have your speedometer calibrated after putting new or oversized tires on your car. New and oversized tires are known to affect the accuracy of your speedometer.

Remember, too, that the older your car is, the more likely the speedometer will be off.

Proof of Insurance

Make sure you keep proof of insurance in your car with you at all times. It's a good idea to keep a copy of your insurance card in the glove compartment. Keep another copy of the card in your wallet. You may also want to photocopy the policy to show that you are insured, because most insurance ID cards typically name only the main insured (your parents, if you are covered under their policy).

Driving without insurance is an offense in most states. In some jurisdictions, your car may be impounded. In others, you might be able to bring proof that you were insured at the time of the incident. Some courts may even allow you to show proof that although you were not insured at the time of the incident, you have subsequently attained insurance. Acceptable proof of insurance should include the name of the insurance carrier, the policy number, effective dates of coverage, and the name of the person who received the citation and/or the vehicle listed on the citation.

> **Tip**
>
> Keep a copy of the face sheet of the insurance policy along with the ID card in your car. This is proof that you are insured under your parents' policy.

Proof of Forged Citation

In rare cases, a sibling, family member, or friend may be stopped by an officer and give your name and personal information, forging your signature on the ticket. If you claim you never received and signed a ticket, bring documentation to prove that the signature is not yours (i.e., other valid documents with your signature) and/or other proof that you were somewhere else at the time of the citation. If you can't prove your whereabouts at the time of the citation, look at the citation closely and see if there is information about you that is incorrect. Did the officer note that the person who signed the ticket had a tattoo or other identifying marks? If you have no tattoos, this may be a way of showing it wasn't you.

If you have any idea who might have used and forged your name, don't be afraid to tell the judge the name of that person and the nature of your relationship. You are not "ratting out" the person who pretended to be you. You are making things right.

Who Do I Bring to Court?

I learned the hard way that I was not the only one affected by my decisions, but also my family.

Parents and Legal Guardians

Your citation will indicate that you are a juvenile, and that you must be accompanied by a parent or **legal guardian**. "Parent" means your mom or dad only. "Legal guardian" means someone appointed by a court or authorized by your parents to be your guardian. This authorization must be in writing.

MYTH: I can appoint a guardian to come with me to court.

MYTH BUSTER: You can't appoint your older boyfriend, dad's girlfriend, or well-meaning aunts, uncles, cousins, older friends, and so on to be your legal guardian for the purposes of court, curfew, or medical matters.

One parent is sufficient for the purposes of court, but both parents will always be welcomed and their presence presents a strong family unit. You might be afraid to tell your parents and be tempted to avoid telling them by bringing a stand-in to court. Don't do it. You'll just be ordered to come back, and you'll have wasted the court's time, your time, and the time of the person you brought along to court. The court checks identification and will note on your case record who accompanies you to court. It's a bad idea to fabricate that your parents are on some extended vacation out of the country when they're not.

Sam B. experienced this when he checked in with the clerk for his trespassing citation. He brought his older brother along, claiming his parents were out of the country for two months and could not be contacted. His claim was noted on the court file. He was told to return with a parent or a verified authorization from his parent. Sam and his parent appeared in court twenty-four hours later. What he didn't realize was that his fabrication affected his credibility at court.

Even if you don't get along with your parents or you aren't currently living with them, they are still legally responsible for your welfare and are obligated to appear in court with you. Kristin M.'s father was deceased and her mother didn't want to have anything to do with her, refusing to come to court and letting a neighbor care for her. Kristin's mother was ordered into court, and a social worker was assigned to the family due to her initial refusal to cooperate.

In David L.'s case, both parents were incarcerated in state prison and he was living with his aunt. But his aunt didn't have any guardianship papers over David. The court continued the case so that David's aunt could request written guardianship from David's imprisoned parents, which she did.

If you turn eighteen in the time between your citation and your court date, some courts will allow you to appear without a parent.

Emancipated Minors

If you are emancipated, meaning you've been granted by a court a release from parental authority and are considered an adult for certain legal purposes, you may come to court without a parent, but you must bring documentation that proves your **emancipation**. When you are emancipated, your parents are no longer responsible for you and you do not have to answer to your parents.

MYTH: I'm emancipated from my parents if I don't live with them or if I have a job.

MYTH BUSTER: Children can't "divorce" their parents. Running away isn't a legitimate way to become emancipated. Emancipation is a legal process overseen by a judge. In almost all cases, emancipation requires parental consent, as well as a finding by a judge that you can support yourself and that it is in your best interests to be emancipated.

Minors in Foster Care or Placement and Other Temporary Guardians

If you are a foster child or live in a group home or have been placed by a court with a family member due to a finding of abuse or neglect, your relative, social worker, or a verifiable placement worker who knows you and your case history should come to court with you. A transportation worker from your placement who isn't familiar with your history won't be sufficient. Relatives who have been granted temporary custody by a court should bring court documents proving temporary guardianship.

Tip

A written authorization should be signed and either notarized or be attached to a legible photocopy of your parents' ID. If your parents cannot attend for work related reasons, bring a letter from their employer verifying the reasons. If the reason your parents cannot attend is medical in nature, bring a letter from the doctor describing the reason your parents are unable to attend.

If your parents cannot attend because they are verifiably out of town or out of the country, are hospitalized or sick, or are unable to leave their jobs, they can appoint a temporary guardian for court, but they must prepare a written authorization for you to bring to court at the time of your first hearing.

Witnesses

Don't bring your witness(es) to your court **arraignment**, or your initial appearance in court. Witnesses will only be heard after a not guilty plea has been made, and at a later date sworn in at a trial.

Other Things to Consider

Do I Need to Hire an Attorney?

Whether or not to hire an attorney is something you should discuss with your parents. Your need for an attorney—and your ability to retain one—will depend on the severity of the offense, the likelihood of a license suspension or other disposition, and your family's finances. Many cases heard in juvenile court relate to infractions and misdemeanors and are heard without attorneys.

If you're unsure as to whether to hire an attorney, you can check with your local **bar association** or the American Bar Association (ABA) for referrals to attorneys who specialize in juvenile, family, or criminal law.

Affidavit of Prejudice

If you believe that the judge before whom you'll be appearing is or might be prejudiced against you for some reason—for example, if the judge has heard other cases against you—you may file an **affidavit of prejudice** and ask that another judge hear your case. In some states, and in some circumstances, you may have to delineate the exact reasoning behind your assertion of prejudice. Other times you might be able to file such an affidavit without stating your reasoning, but if you do so, you may request a change of judge only once.

Conflict of Interest

It's not appropriate for the judge to hear or consider any matter in which she has an interest. A judge may not handle any matters that involve family, friends, or former clients. In those cases, the judge should **recuse**, or disqualify, herself and transfer the case to another judicial officer.

CHAPTER 4

Coming to Court for My Hearing

I can't believe I am here right now, *I thought to myself as I sat down.*

Waiting for my court appearance was very stressful because I was worried about the amount of money my parents would have to pay. And when the court date finally arrived, I remember saying a prayer before my appearance before the judge.

While I was in the courtroom, my palms were sweaty and I had not a clue about what to do, what to say, with an overwhelming sense of guilt running through my body.

Today I came to court and felt very scared. I thought I was going to be arrested and put in jail.

The day you've been waiting for and probably worrying about for weeks has finally arrived. It's only natural for you to be concerned about what might happen during your hearing, but try to look at this time as a learning experience that will, whether you know it or not, actually give you some new life skills. These skills include navigating a bureaucracy, researching information, asking questions of friends and family, and planning.

Preliminaries

Arrive on Time

If your citation specifies a certain time, make sure to arrive on time. You can usually find directions to the courthouse on the court Web site or do a MapQuest or Google search. Leave plenty of time for driving, parking, and a weapons search. Many urban courthouses have weapons-screening devices. To avoid delays, don't bring any contraband to court. If you arrive late, your case may be continued to another day.

Expect a line. Depending on the time of your hearing, your wait might be long, but if you've come for an 8:30 a.m. hearing, most courts will try to get you out of there by noon at the latest.

Signing a Statement of Rights

Most courts provide a form called a **statement of rights**, which you must read and sign. As with your ticket, signing this form does *not* mean you are admitting guilt; it only confirms that you understand what your rights are. Make sure to read it and any other forms you might be given carefully. Don't just sign something because the clerk asks you to do so; understand what you're signing, what your specific rights are, and what rights, if any, you are waiving.

In some courts, the statement of rights is handed out en masse to all the defendants present. This might also be done by video or

> A statement of rights might typically include information on
>
> 1. your right to an attorney;
> 2. your privilege against self-incrimination;
> 3. your right to a trial;
> 4. your right to call witnesses; and
> 5. your right to an appeal after a trial.

audiotape, along with an explanation of court procedure. After reading and signing the form, the judge will generally ask you if you've read or heard and understood your rights.

Consolidated or Companion Cases

If you were cited with other people for the same offense, they may be heard by the court together as **consolidated cases** for efficiency's sake. It's often helpful to hear all the facts relating to one incident at the same time. So don't be surprised if you're called in to court along with the people who were cited with you.

What Does the Courtroom Look Like?

You've probably seen courtroom dramas on television or at the movies. Most courtrooms are set up in much the same way—the judge's area, or "bench," is elevated somewhat, behind which is the state seal. There are both U.S. and state flags on either side, along with additional work stations for the court reporter, clerk, bailiff, interpreter, and so on. Not all juvenile courtrooms, however, are the large courtrooms you see on television. Some are smaller **hearing rooms**, designed and built specifically with juveniles in mind.

Depending on the court, you may be sitting with your parents, or your parents may be asked to sit behind you.

Body Language, Dress, and Demeanor

I really apologize for the attitude that I gave. I really am just nervous. I'm trying to change and I really want to be somebody big in my life, but it's just hard for me.

I don't follow the rules because I just don't. I don't know how to explain it. I know my attitude will just make this ticket worse for me, but I will deal with it.

Both you and your parents should dress appropriately for court. Don't wear grungy clothing that makes you look like you've just stepped out of a construction zone. Clothing bearing drug- or alcohol-related themes or promoting drug use are considered inappropriate, as are T-shirts with skeletons or those that contain expletives. A jacket and tie or a dress aren't usually required, but do go a long way in telling the judge you care. Don't wear beach clothing, shorts, flip-flops, tops that show your midriff, and the like. Don't wear what is commonly considered gang attire—sagging pants and baggy white T-shirts. Sunglasses are not allowed unless medically approved. Don't wear a hat, hood, cap, or headdress, unless it is for a religious purpose. Chewing gum, cameras, and cell phones are also not permitted.

Don't waste your and your parents' time by being sent home for improper dress. Sergio L. wore a cutoff T-shirt to court. When he was told he couldn't appear before the judge and would have to return with proper attire, his mom made him wear her sweater as a cover-up. Frank R. wore low-riding jeans that were practically falling off. He was sent home and came back to court with different jeans—that were also three sizes too big. After two hours spent going back and forth, his mother eventually found the belt he was hiding in his backpack.

Your behavior in the courtroom or even in a waiting room is indicative of your credibility and character. It's not a good idea to belittle or demean the clerk or bailiff, throw papers, or pound your fist on the counter. The clerk or bailiff can be your best friend or worst enemy, and being polite will go a long way in expediting your case. You may be nervous or excited, but try not to interrupt when someone is talking to you. While in court, remain seated quietly and wait for your turn to speak.

Something to Think About

You wouldn't wear cut-off shorts to an interview for a job you really wanted, would you? Think of your court hearing as a job interview. Baggy pants and midriffs look cool on MTV, but are they really appropriate for court?

> Attitudes that don't work:
>
> I'm-really-mad-about-being-here look
> You-can't-tell-me-what-to-do look
> I'm-taking-all-AP's-so-I'm-smarter-than-you look

Talking back or rolling your eyes at court personnel, the judge, or your parents will only serve to show the judge you don't understand—or don't want to understand—the seriousness of your situation.

You will have the opportunity to explain your circumstances, but you should be prepared to do so productively, without attitude. For example, if the judge suspends your license, you may *want* to lash out with, "But how am I going to get to work?" A better approach, though, might be: "I understand why you've suspended my license, but can I please explain what is going on in my life, and could you please consider a restricted license instead of a suspended one?"

If you have questions, write them down ahead of time. You'll only have one short opportunity to see and talk to the judge.

"Your honor," "Ma'am," or "Sir" is the proper way to address the judge, but any effort to speak calmly, succinctly, and respectfully will be appreciated.

Your words and your demeanor should show that you care and that you're sorry. Showing remorse may make the difference between a sixty-day and ninety-day suspension of your license in a traffic case, and the difference between fifty hours of community service or twenty hours in a misdemeanor offense. You can display your remorse by talking about it while you're in court, or, if you feel more comfortable, in a letter you've written ahead of time to present to the judge.

Your Parents' Role

Your parents are there to support you, but expect them to answer the judge's questions honestly. And just as you can present a letter to the judge, so can your parents. Your parents know you best, and their input is valuable to the judge hearing your case. Most judges will give your parents an opportunity to tell the court something about you, such as any relevant history of problems, recent trauma, death in the family, accidents, or learning disabilities, and so on.

> Dear Judge:
> My son can't be in any school because there are always problems that result in expulsion. He has an attitude with everyone, including teachers whom he screams and fights with. He also fights with other students. He smokes marijuana and does inappropriate things like take things that are not his. I have found pipes in the house. His behavior at home is sometimes violent toward his siblings. I am asking you to help me.

> Dear Judge:
> I personally welcomed the ticket our son had been issued because it helped me to reinforce some of the difficult choices he must make in a society where many of the friends he has been close to since preschool and grade school are now making stupid choices with life-and-death consequences.

> Dear Judge:
> I am in the sad position of having to teach my daughter a lesson about authority and the criminal justice system. This is because you gave her the same sentence for possession of a graffiti implement that you gave the other girl, who, although she was not cited for tagging, admitted to doing so. This sentence, far from helping her become a good citizen, is going to make her cynical.

Who Will I See in Court?

Clerk

The clerk is the right arm of the judge, the person who prepares, finds, files, and attends to all the paperwork associated with your case. The clerk also collects fines, which in some instances you may be permitted to pay at a counter without seeing the judge.

Bailiff

The bailiff is the person in charge of security in the courtroom. This is usually a deputy sheriff, armed and in full uniform.

Counselors

Some courts may have counselors on hand to speak with you before or after your hearing. The judge may also want to confer with them before making a decision in your case.

School Liaisons

Your local court may have a school liaison who acts as a bridge between the court and your school. She may ask for school records, be in touch with your own school counselor or dean, or help in finding a school for you if you have special needs.

Probation Officers

Many juvenile courts have probation officers. A probation officer conducts an investigation into the background of a minor and provides the judge with the result of that investigation. The probation officer will make recommendations as to sentencing. This could be in the form of a recommendation for conditional discharge, formal probation, or commitment to a youth prison. After sentencing, the probation officer also follows up on the minor's progress with regard to school or other probation orders, and informs the court if the minor has violated probation.

Prosecution

The case/citation may be prosecuted by a **district attorney** (also known as DA) or **city attorney**, or, in more informal settings, a judge or probation officer alone.

Will There Be a Jury?

Just like in family law matters, such as divorce and child custody cases, there is no jury or right to a jury trial in juvenile cases. That means it is solely up to the judge to make decisions in your case.

The only time your case might be decided by a jury is if a determination has been made that you are unfit to be tried in juvenile court and your case is transferred to adult court. Every state has its own criteria as to what age and what particular types of crime make an offender unfit for juvenile court.

Judge

The person who presides over the case is a judicial officer, sometimes also called a bench officer. Different jurisdictions may use different names, so you might be seeing a judge, commissioner, referee, magistrate, or hearing officer. Juvenile Court judges are usually granted wide discretion in hearing and making dispositions in your case.

In some jurisdictions, you may be able to find out ahead of time who will be hearing your case; in others you won't. Generally, you can learn something about a judge by looking up her profile on your local court's Web site or in the archives of your local legal newspaper. In Los Angeles, the *Metropolitan News* and the *Daily Journal* serve as the city's legal newspapers. Other daily, weekly, and monthly legal newspapers in the U.S. include *Pennsylvania Law Weekly*, *Massachusetts Lawyers Weekly*, *New York Law Journal*, and *New Jersey Law Journal*.

Interpreters

If your parents don't speak English or you're a new immigrant and don't feel comfortable communicating in English, you have a right to request an interpreter. Courts in multicultural cities have interpreters on hand for many languages, including sign language interpreters. If your language is not in common usage in your state, an interpreter may have to be ordered for you for another day. Remember—it's your and your parents' right to fully understand and engage in the proceedings.

The Arraignment

What Is an Arraignment?

The arraignment is the initial hearing at which the judge will inform you of the charges against you by reading off your citation and then ask you to enter a **plea** to the charges. An arraignment is not a trial where arguments for a case are heard. If you're under a certain age (fourteen in California, for example, but the age varies from state to state) the judge must first determine if you understand the wrongfulness of your behavior. The judge might do that by asking you questions such as "Did you understand that what you were doing was wrong?" or "Do you understand why you are here in court today?"

The judge will then formally request your plea by asking, "How do you plead?" or ask you if the allegation—what the officer claims you've done—is "true or not true."

You may respond with any of the following:

1. Guilty
2. Guilty with an explanation
3. Not guilty
4. No contest
5. True or Not True.

No contest (from the Latin words **nolo contendere**) is an admission of guilt and has the same legal effect as a plea of guilty, but cannot be used as an admission in other proceedings. For example, a no contest plea with regard to a ticket for no left turn that also involved an accident could not be used against you in civil proceeding relating to the same accident.

If you plan to contest the citation, don't bring diagrams, photos, maps, or witnesses to your arraignment. Leave that for trial, as the officer who cited you to court will not be present at an arraignment. He is called to court only if you request a trial.

If, on arraignment, you are still not sure as to how to plead, you can ask the judge for a continuance or request a few extra minutes to decide on your plea. Understand, however, that this request is not always granted; this will depend on the jurisdiction and the particular judge.

You may also request an **indicated sentence**, meaning that you ask the judge what type of sanction or fine she normally imposes in similar cases before you make your plea. Again, you should understand that this request is not always granted.

Pleading Guilty or No Contest

If you plead guilty or no contest, the judge will proceed to the **disposition** phase of the hearing, that is, he will make a decision as to the fine, orders, and consequences you will receive.

Don't plead guilty just because you want to get it over with or because you think it's a hassle for you or your parents to appear in court again for a trial. Although these practicalities are a consideration, they should be only a part of your decision-making process with regard to your plea. Similarly, don't be talked into a trial by your par-

Tip

Think carefully about how you want to plead. You get one opportunity to make your plea and you should consider these factors:

1. Do you have a legal or factual defense?
2. Do you feel responsible for the acts you've committed?
3. Is the time and effort it would take to return to court for a trial worth it for you and your parents?

ents. Your parents' guidance is important and valuable, but it is your responsibility and your record that is at stake, not theirs.

After a plea of guilty or no contest, expect the judge to ask questions of both you and your parents. These questions can relate to previous problems at home or at school, disciplinary or otherwise, and efforts to resolve these problems, as well as questions about how you are doing in school. The judge might ask you *why* you committed the offense. This is not an intrusive question, but is designed to help the judge construct a proper disposition (order) in your case.

Remember, too, that the judge will have a copy not only of this citation, but also your entire record of citations, to help him devise a disposition for your case. This means that if you've had previous speeding tickets, or a history of fighting at school or truancy, he will know, and this will impact his decision.

Your Right to a Speedy Trial

If you plead not guilty, you have a right to a **speedy trial**—usually anywhere from forty-five to sixty days from the day you make your plea. (Check your local codes for the specific guidelines in your jurisdiction.) If you want to postpone the trial to a more convenient time for you or your witnesses, you may ask for a continuance with the court's permission. The court will ask you to sign a **time waiver**, where you relinquish your right to a speedy trial.

Requesting a Change of Venue

In certain, special cases and if the rules of court allow, you also might be able to request a trial in a different **venue**, or a different courthouse than the one you were cited to. Some jurisdictions, for example, will allow you to appear in the courthouse closest to your home address; others will not.

Your Trial

Your trial is your opportunity to present your case. It is the time when the court will weigh the reliability and credibility of the testimony it hears. You and the officer who cited you (and any witnesses) will be asked to raise your right hand and swear or affirm to tell the truth. You've probably heard this question or some variation of it in movies and on TV:

> Do you swear that the testimony you are about to give this court is the truth, the whole truth, and nothing but the truth?

Although saying these words may sound a little dramatic to you, understand that your obligation is to answer truthfully. **Perjury**, or lying under oath, is an additional offense.

Tip

Telling the truth is not only the right thing to do, but it also works in your favor from a practical point of view. Lies and exaggerations are almost always eventually found out and can only work against you with regard to your credibility. Lying to others means you're also lying to yourself.

Documents, Diagrams, and Photographs

Your trial is when you bring documents, diagrams, and maps to court. Some courtrooms are supplied with chalkboards, but don't assume these will be available. Some courts allow video evidence, but check with the clerk first. Simple diagrams can be helpful and although they don't have to be drawn to scale, they should accurately reflect the area depicted. Christine S., for example, came fully equipped with a to-scale poster board illustration of the intersection in question and miniature Matchbox cars to her trial for a stop sign ticket. This isn't necessary, but the court allows you to be as creative as you wish, within reason.

Photographs should fairly represent the situation that existed at the time of the citation. **Hearsay evidence**, meaning oral or written statements of people who are not in the courtroom, is not usually considered by the judge because the judge or prosecution cannot **cross-examine**, or question, the person who made the statement.

Because the **burden of proof** is on the officer, she will speak first, outlining her experience, duty assignment, and a narration of the events that led up to the citation. The judge may ask some questions of the officer, such as:

1. Whether the officer has **independent recollection** of the incident, that is, whether she remembers the incident apart from reviewing or reading off her notes of the citation.
2. Whether the officer can positively identify you as the person to whom the citation was issued.
3. Whether the officer can attest to the court's copy of the citation by verifying her own signature on the citation.

You will then be given an opportunity to question the officer. If you have no questions, you can proceed directly to making your own statement.

Alicia G.'s father was a member of the Los Angeles Police Helicopter Unit. He brought aerial maps of a stop sign that Alicia was alleged to have not stopped at. Sounds good, right? Wrong. Alicia's father used city monies and equipment inappropriately, and the aerial photos actually showed that Alicia stopped at the wrong spot.

Tip

Prepare yourself for court. Read up on the code section and give some thought as to how you can efficiently and effectively present your case. Judges are happy to see minors who have turned the incident into a learning experience. But don't overdo it. Overkill doesn't always help. Also, avoid repeating yourself and don't argue with the officer. Remember, you are presenting evidence to the judge, not to the citing officer.

Trial Witnesses

The witnesses you bring to your trial must base their testimony on their personal knowledge. Keep in mind that your friends may not be the best witnesses for you. I've seen well-intentioned witnesses ruin their friend's cases by saying the wrong thing. Consider who your witnesses are and how articulate they are. If your witness is a fourteen-year-old passenger who doesn't have a license, how credible or convincing do you think she will be as a witness in a traffic-related case?

Here is an example of what an exchange with a typical teen witness might sound like:

"I don't think my friend was speeding."
"How do you know that?"
"It didn't feel like she was speeding."
"Did you look at her speedometer?"
"Uh, no."
"Do you have a license to drive?"
"Uh, no."
"What were you doing?"
"I was in the back, listening to music."

In the course of the trial, the court will delve into your witnesses' relationship with you, and if they are simply trying to be helpful just because they are your friends, their testimony will not help your case.

You should make arrangements to bring your own witnesses and make sure they appear for the trial on time. Remember, too, that you can discuss the case with your witnesses, but you shouldn't tell them what to say.

Trial Continuance

Both you and the officer who cited you usually have an opportunity to ask for a continuance. It is up to the individual court to determine whether the request for continuance is reasonable and justifiable. Requests are usually granted in cases of hospitalization, sickness, family emergency, and the like.

MYTH: If the officer doesn't appear in court, my case will be dismissed.

MYTH BUSTER: If the officer doesn't appear in court, your case will *probably* be dismissed in most cases, but don't count on it. Be prepared for the case to be continued to another date if the officer or other witnesses have notified the court of some legitimate reason for the absence.

Your Failure to Appear at Trial

If you fail to appear at trial, the court might conduct a **trial in absentia**, or in your absence. When this happens, the court takes testimony from witnesses and makes a finding of guilty or not guilty without your presence.

Top Ten Excuses

If you're thinking about using one of these, you might want to think again.

1. "I was holding it for a friend."
2. "I did it because of peer pressure."
3. "I don't know why I did it."
4. "The cop only stopped me because I'm driving a nice car."
5. "I wanted to see how it feels."
6. "I wasn't thinking straight."
7. "I was going with the flow of traffic."
8. "It was a phase."
9. "I found it on the street."
10. "I was at the wrong place at the wrong time."

Right to Appeal

Once a determination or finding of guilt has been made by the judge, you have a right to **appeal** the ruling either via **rehearing** or directly to an appellate court using appeals procedures defined in your state or local laws. Keep in mind that the right to appeal a judge's ruling is always limited in time. You may have as little as ten days to file your appeal.

CHAPTER 5

Driving, Pedestrian, Bicycle, and Related Violations

I love being able to drive and I love the independence that has come with it.

I do agree that the license age should not be legal until age eighteen, because in this world age sixteen is just too young to be driving. The only thing I don't agree with is the type of punishment that first time offenders receive for a first-time violation. I think it is too harsh and there should be some way to warn teen drivers of the penalties they could face.

Driving Offenses

Getting a driver's license is something most teens look forward to, a milestone that represents growing up and freedom, but with it comes the responsibility for your own safety as well as the safety of others. Driving has become such a normal everyday activity that it's easy to lose sight of the fact that even a 40 mph crash can total a car and land you in the hospital. So consider your traffic citation a wakeup call. After all, it could be worse: The citation you received could have been an accident.

Driving without a License

To drive without a license is dangerous because you can hit someone and could cause an accident and could crash and injure someone.

I disrespected my uncle when I stole his car and betrayed his trust. I risked either crashing [or] damaging something, and the people who were in the car with me could have gotten hurt.

Driving without a license is a misdemeanor for which you may incur substantial fines and penalties. Your car may be towed and impounded and the offense may also affect your ability to obtain a license in the future.

Thirteen-year-old Peter R. often helped his older cousin fix cars. As a reward, the older cousin began teaching him how to drive. One day Peter felt he knew enough about automobiles to drive. Unfortunately, he backed into a parked car. Luckily, he didn't hurt himself or anyone else in the process, but his cousin's car was impounded. The impound fees were high, and the family couldn't afford to recover the car. Fourteen-year-old Rob S. took his grandmother's car to buy some food. He ran a stop sign and collided with a pole and another car. The fire department was called and transported him to a hospital. Luckily, he wasn't seriously injured, but he was cited for driving without a license and

Tip

Most legitimate auto dealerships won't sell a car to an unlicensed driver, but a private party might be willing to sell you a used car from a newspaper or Internet listing, or even on the street. Don't be tempted to throw your money away on this kind of a deal. It's against the law to sell a car to someone who doesn't have a license, and chances are there's something wrong with the car mechanically or with its registration.

was billed for the damages to the city-owned electric pole.

Sixteen-year-old Sasha was unlicensed but wanted to buy a used car. He went on craigslist and contacted a private auto seller who was willing to sell him a car. He was short of money, but the seller allowed him to take the car to get more money. On his way to the ATM he was involved in a highway crash. He was injured, but left the scene and didn't stop to exchange information and check on the passengers in the car he struck. He was cited for driving without a license and hit-and-run.

Tip

However easy it may look, and no matter how many times you've driven a virtual car in video games, driving and controlling a real two-ton car is not the same. It requires maturity, classroom and behind the wheel instruction, and a host of instant reflexes. Older brothers, friends, or cousins who try to be "nice" and let you drive their cars without a license are not doing you any favors.

Marna N.'s parents were immigrants who didn't speak English and didn't drive. When Marna turned sixteen, they bought a car and often asked her to pick up her younger sister from school and shop for them, even though she also didn't have a license. Marna was cited for driving without a license even though she was simply trying to obey her parents. Gerson B. drove without a license because he wanted to take his girlfriend out for her birthday. He was cited for the offense. His girlfriend also broke up with him after spending an evening at the police station because of his offense.

A sad story involved Yoni R. His older brother passed away after a two-year illness and Yoni's mother asked him to help out the family with errands that related to his brother's funeral arrangements. Although the case could not be dismissed, his special situation was taken into account. Instead of paying a fine, he was ordered to participate in family therapy, to make sure he had a safe place to express his sadness and feelings of anger at the loss of his brother.

If you've taken the car without permission, the act may also be considered theft, and the car's owner is entitled to file a stolen vehicle report. This is an additional and more serious offense.

Raul M. was cited for driving without a license. In court he explained, "It was an emergency." When asked what was the emergency, he answered that he had gone to the store to pick up some food. Emergencies, however, are about life and death—such as taking an ill person to a hospital. Anything else—even going to school, work, church, picking up food, or even going to the doctor—is not considered an **exigent circumstance** for the purpose of the offense of driving without a license and is considered only a matter of "convenience."

Tip

It's okay to say "no" to your parents if they ask you to drive for them when you don't have a license. Remember that even if you're just trying to be helpful, driving without a license will go on your record, affecting your ability to get a license and perhaps a job later on. Note also that parents who knowingly allow their unlicensed minor children to drive can also be cited.

Sixteen-year-old Angela G.'s parents were recently divorced. She didn't see her father and often argued with her mother. One night she left the house without permission and went to a rave with four male friends. On the way back, all four of the boys were under the influence of marijuana, so Angela drove, despite the fact that she hadn't even attended driver's educa-

Tip

It's not a good idea for you or your parents to buy you a car before you earn your driver's license. Having a car sitting on the driveway or in the garage waiting for you might be too much temptation.

tion. Unfamiliar with driving on the freeway, Angela missed a transition road, turned suddenly to change lanes, and then lost control of the vehicle, which went up a curb and across the other lanes. The car hit a dirt hill and rolled over, landing on its roof. All the passengers sustained some form of injury.

Tip

One bad decision can easily be followed with others, and can create a domino effect as you scramble to remedy or deal with the consequences of your first bad decision.

Even if you're not driving a car per se, you might still be cited for driving without a license. Fourteen-year-old Johnny S. took his friends for a joyride in his father's golf cart in a gated community. The vehicle flipped over sideways, ejecting the passengers, who were hurt in the accident. Johnny was cited for driving without a license, even though a golf cart isn't technically a car.

You can also be cited for driving without a license even when the car's engine is off. Donald L. was cited for driving without a license when he sat in the driver's seat of a car that had broken down and was being pushed to a gas station. The fact that he was "in control" of the vehicle—steering it—was enough to cite him under the statute, even though the engine was not running. The surrounding circumstances, however, will dictate whether a person who doesn't have a license will be cited for merely steering the car.

Remember, too, that the law doesn't differentiate between a "short" or "long" drive. Moving a vehicle a few feet, even from one side of the street to another, is considered "driving." In addition, most states require a special license or endorsement if you're driving a motorcycle. Driving a motorcycle when you only have a driver's license is deemed **driving out of class** and is considered a violation.

On a lighter side, seventeen-year-old Armen L.'s girlfriend called in the middle of the night and asked him to come over, not because of any emergency but because she was hungry. "I didn't know what I was doing," Armen said in court. When I asked him why, he responded—"You don't understand, I really liked that girl." Maybe if Armen had played hard to get, he wouldn't have faced fifty hours of community service for driving without a license.

Tip

Don't get into a car with someone you don't really know, such as a friend of a friend. Don't be afraid to ask if the driver is licensed to drive. A person who drives without a license shows a reckless disregard for your safety.

Passengers in vehicles driven by teens who don't have a license also have a stronger chance of getting into trouble. Although they can't be cited for a driving offense, they are more likely to be cited for other offenses that might occur while they are passengers in a car driven by someone who is behaving irresponsibly by driving without a license.

In Minnesota, the state legislature enacted a special law with regard to unlicensed teenagers involved in crash-related violations or alcohol and drug violations. The law, called Vanessa's Law (2004), was created in response to an accident in which a teenage passenger was killed in a vehicle driven by an unlicensed fifteen-year-old.

Fake Licenses and Fake Identifications

Your friends will tell you that fake IDs are easy and cheap to get—and they are. Some teens use them to buy cigarettes or alcohol. Others use fake IDs to get into over-twenty-one dance clubs and bars. Don't be tempted. In the post–9/11 climate, the use of fake IDs is taken very seriously by law enforcement. Although using a false driver's license or a fake ID is not a "driving" violation per se, the offense is listed under state vehicle codes.

Remember, too, that if you're carrying around more than one ID, you might flash the wrong one at the wrong time. Betsy R. learned this lesson when she pulled out her fake ID in court instead of her real one. The consequence? Both the real and fake IDs were confiscated by the court.

It's also illegal for you to use or borrow someone else's driver's license or identification or alter your own license to make it appear that you're twenty-one.

Speeding

The videos they showed shocked me. One especially will haunt me forever. There was one story of a mother driving without her seatbelt. The passenger was her sister, and her two young daughters in the back seat. A drunk driver hit her, killing her instantly. What shocked me was that she must have bit down on the steering wheel. The drunk driver was going at such a high speed that the woman's teeth still inside the gums was left on the dashboard.

Maximum and Prima Facie Speed Zones

Speed cases are usually cited under a **prima facie speed** code section or a **maximum speed** code section. The prima facie speed limit is the limit determined by the conditions of the roadway and a speed survey called a **traffic and engineering survey**. (See more about these kinds of surveys below.) Road conditions, weather, and other circumstances, such as time of day or whether pedestrians were present, are factors that can be presented and argued at trial. Radar and laser are used in prima facie speed zones to determine speed.

Maximum speed zones are usually reserved for highway driving, where the maximum speed could be 55, 65, or 75 mph. Any speed over the maximum is a violation without regard to other factors or conditions.

Another kind of speeding ticket is specifically for speeds over 100 mph, a special offense for which the DMV point count can be higher.

Radar and Laser Devices

Trials involving the use of radar or laser may require special proof. Generally, radar devices are radio transmitters/receivers. They transmit a signal at a prescribed frequency, and the signal travels out and is reflected off a solid object. If the object is moving, the transmitted signal undergoes a change in frequency in direct proportion to the speed of the object. The radar converts the change in frequency (Doppler shift) to miles per hour, and the speed is displayed on a screen. Radar is used in both stationary and moving units.

In some jurisdictions, a traffic and engineering survey must be presented to the court as a foundation for the use of radar or laser. These surveys are typically updated or recertified every five to seven years, and include information about the type of roadway, traffic volumes, existing speed zones, and accident rates.

Radar readings can be affected by high-voltage power lines, neon and/or florescent lights, and power surges. Laser devices are considered more accurate as the laser beam pinpoints a specific target car, rather than a larger area that may include more than one vehicle.

Relevant questions or issues you might want to ask at a trial where radar or laser was used are:

1. Can the officer produce a certificate of calibration for the unit?
2. Can the officer produce a traffic and engineering survey of the area warranting the use of radar?
3. Does the officer understand how radar works?
4. Was a tuning fork used to check the external calibration of the radar and when was it last checked for accuracy?
5. Did the officer first determine your speed by estimation?
6. Was there anyone else on the roadway?
7. Were there any obstructions that might give a false reading?
8. Why did the officer believe the speed you were going was unsafe?

Estimation and Pacing

Officers also use **pacing** as a way of determining your speed. Pacing involves placing the police vehicle behind or to the side of your vehicle for a certain distance, usually between a quarter of a mile to a mile, and then using the speed of the police vehicle to establish your speed. If the police officer has paced you, she should bring a verified copy of her vehicle's most recent calibration to trial.

Speed estimation is also considered a valid form of determining speed. Officers learn to estimate speed in special field-training exercises where the target vehicle's direction (either approaching or receding) is noted and then the officer's estimation is tested against a stationary radar or laser unit. By doing this exercise over and over again, the officer becomes proficient at estimating speed. A final test determines the officer's estimation skills and establishes her **average plus/minus error rate**. She should bring that documentation to court at trial or testify as to her score.

Defenses to Speeding

"I was going with the flow of traffic."
Flow of traffic is a frequently offered excuse for speeding, but this isn't usually sufficient as a defense. Your obligation as a driver is to look at your speedometer (which you must maintain to be accurate) and at the traffic control signs indicating speed.

Tip

Don't feel pressured to speed because other drivers are honking at you, or even tailgating you. Choose better options, like pulling over to the side of the road, when dealing with aggressive, speeding drivers.

"My speedometer wasn't working."
If you want to claim that your speedometer wasn't working, bring a certified calibration of your speedometer to court. It won't be sufficient to dismiss your case, but it may be considered a mitigating

factor and give the judge a reason to reduce your fine or allow you to attend traffic school.

"It was an emergency."

Emergency situations—such as someone in the hospital, or an earthquake, blackout, flood, ice storm, or fire—are scary and stressful, but they are not considered good reasons to speed. Speeding to an emergency situation is basically exchanging one dangerous situation for another. Consider that you won't be any help to the person in need if you're hurt while speeding on your way to them. An emergency situation may not be a defense so as to dismiss your ticket, but it may be offered as an explanation in mitigation.

"I was stressed out."

Besides not paying attention to the speed limit, your speedometer, or intentional speeding, there are many other reasons or situations that lead people to speed, including situations such as time management, traffic jams, or telephone calls regarding an emergency circumstance. Elana D., for example, admitted to speeding, explaining that her Obsessive Compulsive Disorder pressured her to be on time to her appointment with her therapist. Although her disorder may have explained her reason for speeding, she was still obligated not to endanger others.

Arthur S. was caught traveling 105 mph in a 65 mph zone. It took the highway patrol five miles to catch up to him. At trial, Arthur claimed he was "only going in the nineties," but he admitted that he had been speeding because he had gotten into a fight with his mom.

Tip

Stay off the road when you're tired, stressed out, frustrated, or have had a fight with parents, siblings, or girlfriends. Take some time to cool off. Your emotions have no business on the road.

"I didn't mean to speed."

Intent is not usually a defense to most garden-variety traffic infractions such as speed, red

Something to Think About

How would you feel if you were speeding and your friends were hurt in your car? How would it feel to face their parents if you survived an accident and their children did not?

lights, stop signs, and the like, because intent is not an element of a traffic offense. It is only an element of the offense and therefore a possible defense if it is clearly designated as such by the specific code (for example, it is unlawful to file a false report of a stolen vehicle "with intent to deceive").

Stop Signs

A stop sign usually requires a three-second, full and complete stop at the limit line painted on the roadway. Note that the stop sign and the limit line aren't always exactly aligned. The stop sign itself warns you that a stop is imminent. The limit line tells you exactly where the stop should be made. Stopping before or after the limit line is not sufficient for the purposes of a violation.

Defenses to Stop Sign Violations

"I couldn't stop because my brakes weren't working."

At first glance, this might sound like a valid excuse, but the fact is that you're responsible for the "reasonable maintenance" of the vehicle you're driving, even if it doesn't belong to you. Once you get behind the wheel of a car, you are responsible for all of its problems, including expired registrations, tinted windows, loud mufflers, and even faulty brakes.

If your brakes failed suddenly, however, you can present the court with a mechanic's letter or receipt of the repair. Have the brakes repaired immediately. If you wait too long to fix the malfunction, it may be difficult to prove exactly when the problem with your brakes actually occurred. It may also indicate that you didn't make a bona fide effort to correct the problem in a timely manner.

Tip

Most stop sign tickets and stop sign accidents occur within a three-mile radius of your house. That's because most people feel overly confident in areas familiar to them and tend to lose focus. It's easy to let your mind drift to what's for dinner as you get closer to your home. Try to pay more attention to the stop signs in your neighborhood.

"I couldn't see the stop sign."
If you're trying to prove that something obstructed your view on the day you received your ticket, make sure you take photographs as soon as possible after the ticket. It is best to take them on the same day, and make sure they're time-stamped, if possible. Don't wait weeks or until the day before you come to court to take them. Conditions can easily change in six to eight weeks—a tree that was overgrown and was obstructing a stop sign could be cut down in the weeks between your citation and your court date. Weather also changes from season to season, and signage can be put up or taken down.

MYTH: If I take lots of photos and present them at trial, my case will be dismissed.

MYTH BUSTER: Photographic evidence can be helpful, but it isn't always perfect proof. Photos can be misleading, depending on what angle you've taken them from. So take at least five photos from different angles.

Street Racing or Speed Contests

I lost many things when they got me for racing. I had my car that I worked hard for. I fixed it and my dad helped me just so I could have a nice, classy looking car. At the end, I lost my car and my license. My dad lost the trust he had for me. I talked to my friends about what I learned and explained everything in detail. To be honest, my friends pictured all of this that I was telling them and they did stop racing on the streets. Now when they want to race their cars, we just go to the track.

Street racing is a dangerous activity that has resulted in the tragic loss of many teenage lives. In many states, if a police officer determines that a person is engaged in a speed contest, he may arrest that person immediately and impound the vehicle.

It's obvious that illegal street racing is an offense. What's less obvious is the fact that merely *watching* an illegal street race can also be a violation. Your presence at a street race may constitute **aiding and abetting**, meaning helping with or promoting, an illegal street race. The best advice is to stay away from any locations where street racing occurs.

Exhibition of Speed

I was being stupid. I just got the car and wanted to feel its power.

Exhibition of speed is a violation commonly known as "peeling out," and is another violation commonly associated with young drivers who like to show off in their car to their friends. Exhibition of speed is a serious safety concern because it makes the tires lose traction, causing the driver to lose the ability to safely control the vehicle. This offense is especially worrisome when there are pedestrians in the area. In many jurisdictions, this offense is considered serious, generating 2 points on a DMV record.

Reckless Driving

Reckless driving is usually an offense characterized by a "pattern" of offenses. It normally requires a willful and "wanton disrespect for the safety of others or property." Speeding alone, even at a high speed, is not usually enough to cite for reckless driving. There must be additional offenses alleged, such as running a red light or a stop sign, for example, along with a high speed.

Lydia D., who was unlicensed, took her boyfriend's truck and was doing "donuts" in the middle of an intersection. When police observed her, smoke was coming out of the back of the truck. Her actions involved several violations and she was cited for reckless driving and arrested at the scene.

Unsafe Lane Change

Unlike violations such as stop signs or no left turns, which are based on a specific act on your part, an unsafe lane change violation is based on an officer's judgment call. If you contest this particular type of violation, your judgment as a new driver is weighed against the judgment of the officer, someone who's had a lot of experience on the road.

Red Lights and Photo Red Lights

Failure to stop at a red light is a common offense, usually stemming from a miscalculation as to the amount of time the light will be yellow. Most yellow caution signals last no more than three seconds.

Photo red lights, or automated traffic enforcement cameras, are being used more and more to snag red light offenders. Although early cameras were deemed unreliable and inconclusive, the newer cameras take at least four photographs, including:

1. the vehicle at the limit line;
2. the vehicle within the intersection;
3. a close-up of the driver; and
4. the front or rear of the vehicle with license plate.

Some jurisdictions also use real-time video for automated enforcement.

This type of citation usually arrives in the mail with a notice to appear and a copy of the photos taken at the time of the violation. There is no observing officer, but there is a **declarant**, an officer who states, "Violation was not committed in my presence. The above is declared on information and belief and is based on photographic evidence."

You have a right to subpoena the declarant for trial. During the trial he will explain how the camera is used, and he should also bring to court the field technician's service and inspection log. He can also explain the numbers noted on the photographs of the intersection, and will bring to court the original photographic evidence. (Your citation will have a color copy of the photograph.) Some jurisdictions also give you a PIN code so that you can view the photographs on a Web site.

Defenses to Photo Red Light Violations

"I was not the driver shown in the photograph."

If you were not driving the vehicle at the time of the violation, you will need to fill out an **affidavit of non-liability**, explaining that you were not the driver and naming the person who was driving the vehicle at that time.

"The photo camera was not working properly."

If you believe the camera was not working correctly at the time of your violation, you must bring documentation to this effect. You could try to research city maintenance records and logs, but this type of research may prove time consuming.

Hit-and-Run

Hit-and-run is a serious offense for which a driver can be incarcerated, depending on the extent of damages and injury. At the very least, the offense affects the individual's driving record for a number of years, making her virtually uninsurable. This violation is committed by both unlicensed and licensed drivers; even licensed teen drivers sometimes bolt from the scene of an accident because they fear having to tell their parents about it.

Felony hit-and-run is a hit-and-run accident where someone was injured. Misdemeanor hit-and-run is a hit-and-run accident in which there was no bodily injury, but there was damage to a vehicle or other entity, such as a telephone pole, wall, gate, and so on.

There is also a subcategory of "noncontact" hit-and-run. When Mandy B. saw that a bicyclist might cross her path, she hit her brakes. The bicyclist also braked, which caused him to fall. By this time, the bicyclist was behind her, and although she saw in her rearview mirror that he had fallen, Mandy assumed that because there was no actual contact between her car and the bicycle, she wasn't obligated to stop and render aid. She was cited for hit-and-run.

Tip

If you are involved in an accident, as the driver you are obligated to:

1. Pull over in a safe place, stop, and render aid, if necessary, or call 911.
2. Calmly exchange identifying and insurance information with other driver.
3. If the other car is parked and you cannot find the owner/driver, leave a note with your identifying information under the windshield wiper or in another appropriate and visible place.

Tina F. claimed she had stopped after getting into an accident with another driver, but the driver began yelling at her and she was afraid to stick around. Fortunately, she had a witness who corroborated her story, but that's not always the case.

DUI

DUI is the well-known acronym for driving under the influence of alcohol or other drugs. Statistics show that teen drivers are more than twice as likely as adults to be involved in a fatal alcohol- or drug-related crash. In California, for example, drivers under the age of twenty-one cannot drive with a blood alcohol content (BAC) of 0.01 percent or higher; drivers age twenty-one and older cannot have a BAC of 0.08 percent or higher. These "legal limits" for BAC are similar all over the country.

> **Tip**
>
> If you're involved in an accident and the other driver becomes unruly or enraged, and you leave the scene for your own safety, you should call the police immediately and make a police report. You should also call your insurance company. Although you should not have left the scene, this will illustrate your intention to live up to some of your obligations as a driver.

If a police officer stops you for driving under the influence, she will usually administer a breath, blood, or urine test to determine your blood alcohol level. If you refuse to take the test, you can face serious penalties. Conviction for DUI doesn't always depend on chemical testing if other evidence is sufficient for a judge to conclude that you were operating a vehicle while under the influence of alcohol or drugs. Penalties include fines, suspension or revocation of driver's license, and even jail time.

U-Turns

Illegal U-turns are commonly made by new drivers who are not yet familiar with certain areas and streets. U-turns are usually legal at business intersections, unless there's specific "No U-Turn" signage. If an area is a mixed use—meaning partially business and partially residential—it's normally considered a business district for the purposes of the U-turn law.

Keep in mind that a U-turn doesn't always have to look like a *U*. Three-point turns can also be considered U-turns.

Failure to Yield to Emergency Vehicles

This offense is often closely related to loud music playing in the car. If your music is too loud, you won't be able to hear police, fire engine, or ambulance sirens in time to properly yield. The offense is also connected to cell phone use while driving, another distraction. Some people panic or become startled and confused when they realize an emergency vehicle is directly behind or very close to them. The key is to be able to hear the siren far enough in advance so that you can properly pull over.

Tip

When you first see the emergency vehicle coming up behind you with its lights flashing, immediately pull over to the right and stop. Make sure you come to a complete stop; do not continue down the road at a slow pace, as the emergency vehicle might have to turn right. Don't speed up and try to stay ahead of the emergency vehicle. If you approach an intersection and notice that everyone else is stopped even though the light is green, slow down and stop. *Never* try to beat an emergency vehicle through the intersection!

Following Too Close

The easy rule of thumb with regard to "following too close" or "tailgating" is to keep one car length between you and the car ahead of you for every 10 miles per hour you're traveling. So if you're traveling 30 mph, for example, keep at least three car lengths between you and the car ahead. If you're traveling 60 mph, leave at least six car lengths.

Stopping Distances

It's important to understand that it takes time to stop a moving vehicle. The car continues to travel (1) before the brakes are applied, while the driver is reacting to a danger (called "thinking distance") and (2) after the brakes have been applied (called "braking distance").

Caravanning

You might often find yourself driving and following your friends' cars to an activity or party. Not knowing your exact destination—

the location or address where the activity will be held—is an invitation to a ticket, because you're basically depending on the car ahead of you to know where you're going. If you're focusing on following the driver ahead of you, it is hard to concentrate on speed limits, road signs, and proper distance between you and the car ahead.

> **Tip**
>
> At 25 mph, your thinking distance is 27 feet and your braking distance is 34.7 feet, for a total of 61.7 feet traveled. At 45 mph, your thinking distance is 49 feet and your braking distance is 112.5 feet, for a total of 161.5 traveled. At 65 mph—the typical speed on a highway—the car travels 71 feet while you're thinking and 234.7 feet while you're braking, for a total of 305.7 feet.

Violating License, Permit, and GDL Restrictions

Restrictions on Your Instruction or Learner's Permit

The minimum age for a learner's permit in nine states is fourteen years old; it is fifteen in thirty others, and the rest require learning drivers to be at least sixteen. Most states require that you take and pass a formal classroom driver education course. These courses are sometimes offered as part of a high school curriculum; otherwise they are available at private driving schools. The number of hours required for classroom education varies from state to state, but typically about forty hours of instruction are required.

> **Tip**
>
> Know exactly where you're going before you leave. MapQuest or GPS navigation systems are great, but even an old-fashioned city map is a good thing to keep in your car.

Once you complete classroom instruction, you may apply for an "instruction" or "learner's" permit for the purpose of on-road instruction and practice. Normally, a driving instructor, licensed parent, or licensed person over a specified age must be in the car with you if you are driving with a learner's permit. Thereafter, a teen driver might be issued a provisional license (California), an intermediate license (Washington State), or a limited-use or full-use junior license (New York State).

Permits, provisional and intermediate licenses, and junior licenses may be suspended, restricted, or revoked if you violate the specific restriction associated with your license.

Restrictions on Your Graduated Driver Licensing (GDL)

Car crashes are the leading cause of death for teens. Because of this sobering fact, thirty-four states have developed some form of graduated driver licensing program. The thinking behind GDL is to allow new drivers to gain driving experience under lower-risk conditions. According to a study conducted with State Farm Mutual Automobile Insurance Co. that appeared in the March 2008 edition of the *Archives of Pediatrics & Adolescent Medicine*, the risk of death for kids riding with drivers aged sixteen to nineteen was at least double that of those riding with drivers aged twenty-five and older.

The GDL often includes (1) an extended learner's permit period of supervised driving; (2) a minimum number of hours of adult supervision during the learner permit period; (3) restrictions on late-night driving during the initial months of license; (4) restrictions on transporting teen passengers during the initial months of license; and (5) seat belt requirements for drivers and passengers. In California, for example, for the first year a teen is licensed, he may not carry passengers under the age of twenty in his vehicle and may not drive past 11:00 p.m.

The statistics seem to bear out the need for GDL. According to the National Highway Traffic Safety Agency (NHTSA) about six thousand teenagers die each year in motor vehicle crashes. Car crashes are the leading cause of death among American teenagers. About 50 percent of teenage crash deaths occur on weekends and after 10:00 p.m. Fifty-nine percent of teenage passenger deaths occur in vehicles driven by another teen. Teenage accidents have gone down significantly since the passage of laws requiring GDL and imposing first-year driving restrictions.

Seatbelts, Child Car Seats, and Unlawful Riding

Seatbelts

Seatbelts are proven lifesavers and should be worn at all times while in a moving car or while the engine is running. Don't wait until you're a block from home or until you get on the freeway on-ramp to put on your seatbelt, as some people do. The same thinking applies to taking off your seatbelt at the end of a journey. Most accidents happen within a ten-block radius of your home.

Seatbelt tickets can be given for improper use of a seatbelt, for example, putting the shoulder strap under your arm instead of over it. If there's a documented medical reason that you are unable to put on your seatbelt properly, bring a note from your doctor to court.

Seatbelt tickets can also be given to passengers riding in taxicabs. You might also get a seatbelt ticket if you are the driver and you have a passenger under the age of sixteen who is not wearing her seatbelt.

Child Car Seats

Every state requires children under a certain age, height, and weight to be strapped into a car seat. Like seatbelts, car seats are proven lifesavers. Check your local laws regarding age, height, and weight requirements. As a general rule, rear-facing car seats or infant car seats are required until a child is one year old and weighs twenty pounds,

Tip

Even a short car ride with a child to the supermarket requires a car seat. If your (or someone else's) baby is fussing in the car seat, you should stop the car and attend to her needs rather than allowing her to be in a moving car outside a car seat.

car seats are required until a child is four years old and weighs forty pounds, and booster seats are required until a child is eight years old and weighs eighty pounds.

Unlawful Riding

Unlawful riding includes riding in the back of a pickup truck or flatbed, standing up in a car through a sunroof, riding in the trunk of a car, or leaning out through the windows. All these kinds of unlawful riding may seem cool on *Jackass* or YouTube, but in reality they are dangerous and are "ticket magnets"—especially in well-known Spring Break vacation areas. Don't take a chance by engaging in this type of unlawful riding, which may land you and your friends in a hospital—or worse.

> **Tip**
>
> If your friends become unruly in the car, take off their seatbelts, and/or hang out of windows or sunroofs, pull over and stop the car as soon as it's safe. It's not always easy to control your friends, but if you turn off the engine and insist that you won't drive until they comply, there's a better chance that they'll listen.

It's not only the passenger who rides unlawfully who can receive this kind of ticket. If you're a driver who allows people to engage in this kind of conduct in your car, you're also liable to get a ticket.

High-Occupancy Vehicle (HOV) or Carpool Lanes

High-occupancy vehicle lanes are special lanes designated for cars carrying more than one person. These lanes were conceived in order to promote and encourage carpooling, and driving solo in an HOV lane isn't typically considered a "moving violation" for which you would receive a DMV point. This type of ticket does, however, generate a hefty fine. On the other hand, crossing over the double-yellow markings into or out of an HOV lane is considered a moving violation for which you would receive a point.

Cell Phone and Text Messaging

Many states are adopting new regulations to restrict cell phone use and text messaging in cars, unless the phone allows hands-free use and is being used in that manner. These new regulations were enacted to reduce the distraction caused by using and holding a cell phone while operating a vehicle.

Look closely at these laws being enacted in your state. There may be special rules in your jurisdiction that relate to drivers under the age of eighteen. In California, for example, as of July 2008, minors can't use *any* form of cell phone while driving, even the hands-free variety.

Equipment Violations and Illegal Modifications

Equipment violations may include mechanical problems involving brakes, lights, (headlights, turn signals, brake lights, license plate lights), horns, mufflers, mirrors, reflectors, tires, windshields, windows, and safety belts.

Illegal modifications include alteration or removal of air pollution emissions control devices, modification of vehicle ground clearance ("lowered" or "raised" vehicles), removal of mufflers and other sound-control devices. They also include unlawful lights such as neon lights under your car or blue-and-red lights that might be mistaken on the road for law enforcement vehicles. Equipment violations and illegal modifications should be corrected after receiving the ticket and before your court appearance, and proof of such correction should be presented to the court.

Tip

You might want to own a cool, decked-out car, but consider the strong probability that your modifications or additions will result in a ticket.

Headsets and Loud Music

A person driving a car (or bicycle) can't wear a headset or earplugs that cover both ears. This means that you can't use your iPod or MP3 player while you're driving a car or riding a bike. The usual exception to this rule involves people engaged in the operation of construction equipment or trash collection and persons operating authorized emergency vehicles.

MYTH: I can't get a ticket for loud music if I don't have special amps in my car.

MYTH BUSTER: You can get a ticket for loud music even if you have a stock radio, factory speakers, and no special amps.

Tickets for loud music aren't generated because loud music is a nuisance. The reasoning behind this kind of ticket is safety. If your music is too loud, you won't be able to hear emergency vehicles (fire, police, ambulance, etc.) until it's too late.

Final Thoughts on Safe Driving

Safe driving includes taking into consideration road, weather, and other conditions. Basic speed laws provide that no person should drive a vehicle at a speed greater than is "reasonable or prudent having due regard for weather, visibility, the traffic on, and the surface and width" of the street, as well as whether there are

Tip

Pay close attention to weather and road conditions. Don't be embarrassed to pull over if it's raining or snowing too hard for you to see the road. Make sure you have your car checked out regularly. This includes brakes, lights, oil changes, and speedometer calibrations.

pedestrians, bicyclists, joggers, or children in the area. Speeding where children are present on a foggy day is obviously more serious than speeding on an empty road where the conditions are clear and dry.

Pedestrian Tickets

> **Tip**
>
> Try to be prepared for the unexpected. Always have a way of contacting your parents in the event of an emergency. Have a cell phone, calling card, or extra money for a phone call and gas.

Pedestrian tickets are designed to ensure your safety as a pedestrian. You might feel that pedestrian tickets are annoying and unnecessary, but consider this: The National Highway Traffic Safety Administration (NHTSA) statistics show that in 2005, 4,881 pedestrians were killed and more than 64,000 were injured. The fact is that as a pedestrian, you have little or no chance against a car. Pedestrians are required to obey crosswalk signals rather than traffic lights, which are intended for drivers. Only where there are no crosswalk signals should you use traffic signals for guidance. Therefore, where a crosswalk signal indicates "Don't Walk" but the traffic light is green, you should not cross the street.

The crucial moment for a crosswalk offense is the moment you step off the curb and into the street. At that moment, the crosswalk signal must indicate "Walk" or depict a walking person. On the other hand, if you've already begun crossing the street and the crosswalk signal begins to blinks "Don't Walk" while you are crossing, you may proceed to the other side. Don't walk or run back.

Pedestrian tickets can also include crossing outside a crosswalk, walking on the wrong side of the roadway when there is no sidewalk, and running suddenly into the path of a vehicle.

Skateboarding Offenses

I agree with some of the skateboarding laws, but disagree with others. There aren't enough places to skateboard legally.

Many states mandate safety helmets be worn while riding human-powered scooters, skateboards, and roller skates or rollerblades for people under the age of eighteen.

> **Tip**
>
> Talk to your parents about good skateboarding locations or skate parks. They can call ahead to see where skateboarding is permissible. Skateboarding stunts and locations look cool on MTV, but are they worth a ticket in the real world?

Skateboards are outlawed on most private and public property, including city sidewalks and streets, because of both liability and nuisance issues. Many property owners don't want to be liable for injuries occurring on their property and post "No Skateboarding" signs.

Benny H. and two friends entered a closed school campus, despite the fact that the gates were locked and secured and trespassing signs were posted. They chose the location because they "saw it in skateboarding videos." Benny didn't realize that the production company that filmed the video most likely obtained permits to skate and film in that location, while Benny didn't. Benny was charged with trespassing.

You should also find out whether your state or city requires you to wear a helmet and elbow and knee pads, either generally or while at a skate park. Finally, most states outlaw holding onto a moving vehicle while on a bike, skates, or a skateboard.

Bike Offenses

Bike riders must obey most traffic rules that apply to motorists, including red lights, stop signs, and so on. They also have to ride with the direction of traffic, which is always safer than riding against traffic because a head-on collision is more dangerous than a sideswipe with a car. Bike riders also shouldn't ride on sidewalks, which interferes with pedestrians. Pedestrians have the right of way on sidewalks.

In many states, minors under the age of eighteen are required by law to wear helmets when they ride their bikes. Check your local laws. Some areas also require a license to operate a bike; although your state may not require a bike license, a local ordinance may do so. The licensing forms can usually be obtained from your local police department or bike shop.

Other laws that impact bike riders relate to bicycle lanes, hand signals, riding near to the curb, right turn lanes, and carrying passengers on anything other than a permanent bicycle seat. Finally, some jurisdictions disallow riding a bicycle at night without specified lights or reflectors. You should always check your local laws to ensure that you're riding legally.

Related Violations

Motorized Scooters

Many states require that minors be sixteen years old and have a valid driver's license or instruction permit and be wearing a helmet in order to legally operate a motorized scooter. Motorized scooters shouldn't be operated on sidewalks or highways. These types of motorized scooter may have driver's seats but are essentially two-wheeled devices powered by a motor with a floorboard that is designed to stand on when riding.

Littering

In some states it's a misdemeanor to throw anything at or from a moving vehicle, and could be a felony to do so if there's an intent to cause great bodily harm. Also prohibited are littering or throwing lit cigarettes from a motor vehicle. You can also be cited for littering as a pedestrian or as a passenger on a bus or subway.

Blocking the Sidewalk

Citations for blocking the sidewalk are used by law enforcement as a means to disperse juvenile crowds and control gang activity. A typical blocking the sidewalk statute might read:

No person shall stand in or upon any street, sidewalk, or other public way open for pedestrian travel or otherwise occupy any portion thereof in such a manner as to annoy or molest any pedestrian thereon or so as to obstruct or unreasonably interfere with the free passage of pedestrians.

Tip

If you see a large crowd of kids congregating on a public street, you might be curious about what's going on, but it's better to find out later, on your local news broadcast, than to be netted with the others in what may become a law enforcement roundup.

CHAPTER 6

Other Offenses

Non-driving related offenses for which you may be cited include a range of wrongdoing typically committed by teens, such as ditching school, curfew violations, shoplifting, vandalism, fights, and drug and alcohol use. Although many of these offenses start off with poor decision making rather than an outright intent to commit a crime, most of these offenses are considered misdemeanors and can have long-term effects on your record.

Status Offenses

Status offenses are those types of offenses that would not be considered an offense if committed by an adult. The most common status offenses are truancy, curfew, underage consumption or possession of alcohol, and "incorrigibility," which means being impossible to control.

Truancy

If you haven't noticed, truancy is heating up. Teenagers around the globe are doing it not thinking of the consequences. We know it's not right and we do it without thinking. Truancy, as we know it, is a negative act.

I just decided to skip school due to the fact that I thought I wasn't going to get caught. Now I realize that if I continue through this path, I shall be struggling through my life. I want to have the luxury, as many people have, the American Dream, as some people would like to call it.

The first time I started to get into trouble was when I started sixth grade. I met a new friend and I began missing school. One day, I decided to leave and I jumped the fence.

School is just so hard for me; I don't even like trying cause when I do try and I fail that just makes me feel more stupid. That's why I don't try.

Truancy laws restrict juveniles from being outdoors or in public places during school hours. "Outdoors" may include public streets, highways, roads, alleys, parks, playgrounds, amusement and eating places, and vacant lots or buildings. The laws are aimed at increasing school attendance and preventing involvement in delinquent behavior. Statistics show that truancy enforcement is closely related to a reduction in daytime burglary and trespassing rates and that truancy is the number one precursor to other more serious offenses.

Truancy can be committed anytime you're not in school when you're supposed to be. Besides ditching school to go to the mall, the beach, or a kickback party, it also includes (1) coming to school late, (2) leaving early, (3) not checking out with your school administration when you're not feeling well, (4) leaving for lunch or nutrition when you don't have a pass, and (5) not going to a class or required activity.

Most truancy laws will include specific hours wherein truancy is committed—typically, 8:30 a.m. to 1:30 p.m. or thereabouts.

Truancy laws don't usually apply if:

1. you're accompanied by your parent or legal guardian;
2. you're on an emergency errand;

3. you're coming and going from employment, medical illness, or an appointment;
4. you have a valid, school-issued pass or off-campus permit;
5. you're on a sidewalk abutting your own residence; or
6. you're involved in an emergency such as a fire, natural disaster, auto accident, or a situation requiring immediate action to prevent serious bodily harm.

Tip

If you've got a school pass to leave for lunch or nutrition, don't leave it at home. Make sure you have the pass, your school ID, and a note from the teacher/dean/principal if you're leaving school during school hours. Most officers won't accept your claim that you have a pass but left it at home.

Some jurisdictions also allow absences for valid religious training or observances.

Chloe B. and some friends decided to ditch their school's pep rally because it was "lame." Even though they weren't supposed to be in class, they were still required to be on the school's campus, and received truancy citations for leaving school.

Penalties for truancy usually include fines, orders for counseling, community service, and/or a return to court with a perfect attendance record along with good grades.

MYTH: I can't get a truancy ticket on the last day of school before vacation or if I'm a senior and have already been accepted to college.

MYTH BUSTER: There are no exceptions in most truancy laws for these situations. The last school day before vacation, your birthday, Valentine's Day, and after you've been accepted to college are situations when you'll most be tempted to be truant. Resist the temptation.

Many states have incorporated "habitual truant" statutes for which there are special dispositions and consequences. California's Education Code, for example, provides that "any pupil who has been reported as a truant three or more times per school year" can be deemed a habitual truant if an appropriate district officer or employee of the school district has made a conscientious effort to hold at least one conference with the parent or guardian and the pupil himself. Under the code section, habitual truants may also lose their drivers' licenses or may have their licenses delayed.

In some states, parents may also be held accountable for their children's habitual truancy.

Violating School Rules

Every school, whether private or public, has rules. Violations of school rules can also result in citations to court. Public schools are governed by a combination of state laws and local school board regulations. Some rules are unique to the particular school; others are mandated by city, state, or federal law. The following can get you suspended or expelled from school and may land you in court:

1. Threatening to hurt another student or teacher
2. Bringing a real or fake gun, knife, or other dangerous object to school
3. Bringing drugs, alcohol, cigarettes, or drug paraphernalia to school
4. Damaging school property
5. Stealing school, student, or teacher property
6. Using profanity
7. Disrupting school activities
8. Defying a teacher's or dean's authority
9. Sexual harassment or bullying
10. Selling a controlled substance

Curfew

I came back from a football game, then me and my friends went to our buddy's house. Then him and his mother got into an argument and his mom said we couldn't spend the night. On our way home, we got pulled over for being in a racing spot at 2:00 a.m.

Many people think curfews are stupid, and so do I. I was just trying to get home. Is that a big crime?

MYTH: If I'm with an eighteen-year-old friend after curfew, I can't be charged with curfew violation.

MYTH BUSTER: Being with a friend, sibling, or cousin who is eighteen or older won't usually exempt you from getting a curfew ticket. Most curfew laws provide that you must be accompanied by a parent or legal guardian.

Curfew laws are probably one of the most controversial laws applied to teenagers. Originally enacted in the late 1800s to decrease crime among immigrant youth, they were also used during World War II to help parents who were busy helping in the war effort control their children. In the 1970s curfew laws reemerged as a response to the growing juvenile crime problem. The reasoning behind curfew laws is two-pronged—to prevent juvenile crime and to protect youth from victimization. In other words, the goal is to keep so-called bad kids off the streets and to keep so-called good kids out of harm's way.

Curfew proponents maintain that there is statistical evidence that curfew laws cut down on juvenile crime. Detractors claim that the statistical evidence is unreliable and does not prove juvenile crime is reduced when curfew laws are stringently enforced. Critics also believe that curfew enforcement is often ineffective and is an unnecessary conduit of nondelinquents into the criminal justice system. Finally, opponents are concerned with minors' First Amendment right to free association. Despite the criticism, U.S. federal courts have upheld curfew ordinances when they promote social, moral, and physical welfare of minors; are not overly intrusive; and contain properly designated exemptions.

Tip

Don't "meet up" with your friends at night in parking lots, alleys, parks, or recreation areas. Plan your evening outings in advance, with specific times for pick-ups from movies, parties, and other acceptable nighttime activities. Don't make detours on your way home from these activities. Just because you're "sort of" on your way home doesn't mean you are actually on your way home. Be aware that there are periodic sweeps or zero-tolerance crackdown efforts in many urban jurisdictions.

Many states, including Georgia, Minnesota, Ohio, Tennessee, and Texas, have laws that enable local governments to enact curfew ordinances. In contrast, Hawaii has enacted statewide curfew legislation. Most curfew laws, however, are under the jurisdiction of local governments. A 1995 survey of one thousand cities with populations of more than thirty thousand found that 70 percent of those cities had curfew ordinances in place.

In the City of Los Angeles, for example, anyone under the age of eighteen is subject to curfew after 10:00 p.m. on both school nights and weekends. In Clark County, Indiana, a curfew violation is committed when a juvenile under the age of fifteen years is in a public place after 11:00 p.m. In the town of Parker, Colorado, curfew is enforced between midnight and 5:00 a.m. for all youths under the age of eighteen. In some jurisdictions, curfew laws target only repeat offenders or those on probation, not all minors. Other cities impose curfews only on October 30 and 31 to prevent Halloween-related pranks and mischief.

Read your local laws carefully. There may be certain exceptions for participation in lawful employment, or school or religious events. Curfews may also not apply when the juvenile is accompanied by a parent or legal guardian. There may be exceptions specified on weekends. Minors responding to emergencies might also be exempted. Some ordinances allow mobility during nighttime hours for minors who are married, accompanied by certain adults, or traveling with a parent's permission. But your parents' permission to be out after curfew might not necessarily excuse you from curfew laws.

Other curfew laws impose strict curfew in specific zones of the city, usually high-crime or important commercial zones. Austin, Texas, for example, has limited youth activity in the nightclub district of the city.

> **Tip**
>
> If you have a job on a night shift, carry your employment ID card or letter from your employer specifying your hours.

Wendy G. and her friends decided to celebrate her birthday party at a local motel. Although they had limited their guest list, the party was crashed by a lot of uninvited guests, mostly because the location was a motel in an iffy part of town. One of the uninvited guests flashed a laser beam at a police car cruising by the location. The officers stopped to investigate, and the entire party was cited for curfew violation. Wendy's situation could have been easily avoided had she and her friends chosen a better location and planned better security for their party.

Alice B. and her friends were on their way home from a basketball game when they saw a car on fire. The fire department had already been called and the police asked them to disperse, but she and her friends lingered to watch at the scene. They all received curfew tickets. This is a good example of how rubbernecking can get you into trouble.

Viviana L. got into a car with acquaintances she really didn't know very well. They drove around for a while, stopping to pick up other teens, when the car was flagged down by a police officer for a registration offense. It turned out that the car had been stolen, and instead of stopping immediately, the driver drove off with all his passengers in the car, the police in pursuit. The driver was jailed and Viviana and the other teens received curfew tickets.

Abby M. was invited to a party by a friend of a friend. She didn't know who was going to be there and where the party was located exactly, but she really wanted to go out and not stay at home on a Saturday night. At the party, people were drinking and using drugs. Abby became uncomfortable and wanted to leave, but her ride didn't and she was stuck at a party where a fight eventually broke out and the police were called. When the party was dispersed by police, her ride disappeared and the officers cited her for a curfew violation.

Just like other offenses, not all curfew violations are alike. If you're on your way home from a movie ten minutes past curfew, the judge will look at your case differently than if it's 4:00 a.m. and you and your friends

Tip

Never get into a car with people you don't know very well. Don't let your wanting to "go out" with friends at any cost cloud your good judgment. Police pursuits can be very dangerous and end up with people being shot or hurt.

Tip

If you're invited to a party, get as much information about specifics beforehand. Know who's giving it and who exactly will be attending, and understand what kind of location the party will be at. If it's a "flyer" party or "kickback" at some industrial warehouse, it's much more likely that the party will be unsafe or become unruly, and someone will call the police. The same holds true if a large party is being held while parents are out of town.

sneaked out of the house and were roaming the streets with no purpose or destination. Penalties can include fines, orders for counseling, special classes, and/or good grades and attendance at school.

Alcohol and Drugs: Using and Possession

I feel bad because I let my parents down. I've seen a lot of people on the street because of drugs. They ask for money to buy food, or even pick up food from the trash. I don't want to end up like them.

I smoked marijuana on a daily basis. There were a couple of reasons why I smoked weed. The main reason was that I had trouble sleeping. Also, some headaches. But those were just excuses. Hopefully after rehab, I'll be able to live a normal life without weed.

Using Drugs or Alcohol

Teenagers turn to alcohol, marijuana, and other drugs for a variety of reasons—peer pressure, curiosity, depression, and the simple desire to fit in with others in a social context. They also often turn to drugs and alcohol as an escape from problems and issues at home and at school.

Sixteen-year-old Mark F., for example, witnessed both of his father's heart attacks. He was the one who called 911 and watched the paramedics take his dad to the hospital. Following his second heart attack, Mark's father no longer recognized anyone in his family and required around-the-clock care. Mark's grades dropped and he started using marijuana to alleviate the feelings of depression he was feeling about his father.

Although Marina M. had headaches and trouble sleeping, her true reason for using marijuana was related to her own father, who had been addicted to drugs and alcohol for thirty-five years. Interestingly, the year Marina's dad became sober was the year Marina started using drugs. Her father's new sobriety broke a family pattern that Marina subconsciously repeated. Twelve-year-old Brenda T. turned to alcohol after her father was killed by a drunk driver and her mother abandoned her. Thirteen-year-old Lynn P. was cited for possession of marijuana. Soon after, she was hospitalized for expressing suicidal thoughts. Delving into her history, it was discovered that Lynn's mother, who had also been a drug abuser, had committed suicide barely a year before. Prior to her mother's suicide, Lynn periodically smoked marijuana with her. Lynn's use of marijuana was her way of connecting to her deceased mother. Marina, Brenda, and Lynn's conduct were all based on their family histories.

Alison W. was an A student with an abusive boyfriend who beat her up and once even cut her hair off. She went to court and had a restraining order filed against him, but despite the restraining order, Alison felt lonely on New Year's Eve and met him at a party where there was marijuana. She was cited for possession of marijuana and her ex-boyfriend was cited for violating the restraining order against him.

Use or possession of drugs and alcohol are misdemeanors, and penalties can include fines, community service, referrals to alcohol and drug rehabilitation, and loss or delay of driver's licenses.

Alcohol

Alcohol is part of a group of drugs called "downers," which are central nervous system depressants. Downers relax and dull the mind, reduce anxiety, and sometimes induce feelings of well-being. At first, alcohol seems to act like a stimulant, but the more it's ingested, the more its depressant characteristics dominate. Long-term use can cause physical dependency and excessive drinking can slur speech and reflexes. Although not legal for purchase or use under the age of twenty-one, alcohol is easily available.

Alcohol can sometimes be ingested unintentionally. Daniel A. was offered alcohol at school by a friend who had brought it in a sports bottle. Daniel became disoriented and sick, vomiting and losing consciousness. He was transported to a hospital. Later, he didn't even remember that he had fallen down and broken his glasses.

Commonly Used Drugs

> **Tip**
>
> Don't accept drinks from people you don't know. Open containers yourself. If you're at a party, keep your drink with you at all times, even when you go to the bathroom. Don't share drinks, don't drink from punch bowls, and don't drink anything that tastes or smells strange.

Marijuana is also called blunt, weed, dope, ganja, grass, herb, joint, Mary Jane, pot, reefer, sinsemilla, and skunk. It can cause euphoria, slowed thinking and reaction time, confusion, impaired balance, cough and respiratory infections, impaired memory and learning, increased heart rate, anxiety, panic attacks, and addiction.

Cocaine is called blow, bump, C, candy, Charlie, coke, crack, flake, rock, snow, and toot. It can increase heart rate and blood pressure, cause feelings of exhilaration, increased temperature, rapid or irregular heart beat, reduced appetite, heart and respiratory failure, chest pain, nausea, strokes, seizures, headaches, and panic attacks.

Other Drugs

MDMA is also known as Adam, clarity, ecstasy, eve, lover's speed, peace, STO, X, and XTC. It causes increased heart rate, mild hallucinogenic effects, increased tactile sensitivity, empathetic feelings, impaired memory and learning, hyperthermia, cardiac toxicity, renal failure, and liver toxicity.

Oxycodone HCL is also known as Oxycontin, Oxy, O.C., and killer. It helps in pain relief and euphoria, but may also cause drowsiness, nausea, confusion, constipation, sedation, respiratory depression and arrest, addiction, unconsciousness, coma, and death.

Methamphetamines, also known as Desoxyn, chalk, crank, crystal, fire, glass, go fast, ice, meth, and speed, cause increased heart rate and blood pressure, aggression, violence, psychotic behavior, memory loss, cardiac and neurological damage, impaired memory and learning, and addiction.

Inhalants include solvents such as paint thinners, gasoline, glues, gases, nitrates, laughing gas, poppers, snapper, and whippets. These inhalants stimulate and cause a loss of inhibition, headache, nausea or vomiting, slurred speech, loss of motor coordination, wheezing, unconsciousness, cramps, weight loss, muscle weakness, depression, memory impairment, damage to the cardiovascular and nervous system, and sudden death.

Prescription Drugs

Even the use of prescription drugs can be illegal. Using or possessing someone else's prescribed drugs is illegal. In many states, possession of prescription medications in nonprescription bottles is also illegal. Sometimes this can put you in an extremely dangerous situation. Billy F., for example, was found barely conscious after a party. When he was searched, the police found some unknown medications in a nonprescription bottle. The police and hospital officials had to call the local poison control center to determine what kind of pills he'd ingested. Later, after he recovered, he was charged with possession of medications in a nonprescription bottle.

Tip

Stay far away from prescription drugs not prescribed to you. Well-meaning friends who offer you their ADHD drugs for the purposes of studying or drugs for anxiety and depression, pain, weight loss, or any kind of drug cocktail are doing you more harm than good. These drugs are highly addictive, have numerous side effects and drug interactions, and need to be monitored by a physician.

For more information on other commonly abused drugs, their effects, and their potential health consequences go to the Web site of the National Institute on Drug Abuse (www.nida.nih.gov/DrugPages/DrugsofAbuse.html).

What Does "Possession" Mean?

MYTH: If the drugs belong to or were bought by someone else, I can't get into trouble. If I'm not holding the drugs, I can't be cited.

MYTH BUSTER: You don't have to pay for the illegal substance, own it, or even use it. Possession means that you had it. It doesn't even have to be on your person or body, meaning you don't have to be holding it in your hands or in your clothing. If the item or substance is within your reach, it can be considered within your possession.

Tip

If your friends are using illegal substances, just being around them is liable to get you into trouble. If you know your friend is carrying around a baggie of marijuana in his backpack, you may want to reconsider your friendship.

Cynthia P. was in the school bathroom with some other friends who were using drugs. Cynthia wasn't using, but, wanting to be protective of the other girls who were, she grabbed the drugs off the bathroom counter when the school police entered the bathroom. Cynthia thought she couldn't get into trouble because she hadn't bought or used the drugs. She didn't realize that mere possession—even though it was only momentary—could land her court.

Compassionate Use of Marijuana or Medical Marijuana Laws

Marijuana is illegal to use or to possess under federal and most state laws. Several states, however, have adopted legislation permitting certain medicinal use of the drug. The following states have medical marijuana or compassionate use laws: Alaska, California, Colorado, Hawaii, Maine, Maryland, Montana, Nevada, Oregon, Vermont, and Washington. Other states have legislation pending with regard to this specific use of marijuana.

These statutes cover the compassionate use of marijuana for people who are terminally ill, or suffering pain or other kinds of symptoms, who need relief from the chronic symptoms of cancer, AIDS, and other diseases that cannot be eased by legal drugs.

The implementation of some of these laws has been slow because of the continuing federal ban. In California, for example, the first initiative didn't specify how much marijuana a person could grow or possess or outline how the drug would be acquired or transported. Follow-up legislation gave qualified patients the right to possess up to eight ounces of dried marijuana and cultivate up to twelve plants.

Other issues that have arisen in California are the questionable clinics that have cropped up that prescribe marijuana to teenagers. Although there are some legitimate uses of marijuana for particular purposes, be aware that a mere "doctor's note" from one of these clinics may not provide adequate legal justification for marijuana usage. An evidentiary hearing may be necessary before trial to produce evidence that the minor is using the marijuana based on the recommendation and approval of a physician for medical reasons.

Joseph P. had severe gastrointestinal issues all his life and had tried prescribed acid reducers, antidepressants, and other kinds of legal drugs, none of which worked to alleviate his symptoms. He produced evidence of his complete medical history, which made him a good candidate for the Compassionate Use Act. In contrast, sixteen-year-old David C. claimed he had back pain and was taking marijuana to alleviate his pain, but had no evidence of first trying out the usually prescribed pain medications for such back pain before turning to marijuana.

Seventeen-year-old Margarita R. was diagnosed with Tourette syndrome. After consultations with numerous doctors and a host of prescription medications that failed to control her behavior, marijuana was prescribed and seemed to alleviate many of her symptoms. Margarita was also a good candidate for an evidentiary hearing because she could back up her claims regarding marijuana usage with documentary evidence and the testimony of her doctors in court.

Possession of Drug Paraphernalia

Drug paraphernalia can include lighters, matches, Zig-Zag papers, pipes, and any other items modified for the purpose of using drugs, such as modified pens, plumbing pipes, and the like.

Even an apple might be considered drug paraphernalia. A police report described an officer's observation of three young men sitting on a curb in front of a parked vehicle. While driving in their direction, he saw an apple roll under the parked vehicle. Upon making initial contact with the subjects, the officer smelled a strong odor of marijuana. When the officer reached under the parked vehicle, he noticed that the apple had two holes punctured in it. He observed that the appearance of the apple was consistent with its having being used to inhale marijuana and charged all three young men with possession of drug paraphernalia.

Possession and Use of Tobacco/Cigarettes

In most states, the purchase, possession, or use of tobacco is illegal for anyone under the age of eighteen. This includes not only cigarettes, but also what is commonly called tobacco paraphernalia, including lighters, matches, chewing tobacco, cigars, and cigarette papers.

According to the American Red Cross, 390,000 Americans die each year from the effects of smoking. Not only do cigarette smokers have a heightened risk for cancer and respiratory diseases, they also are at more than twice the risk as nonsmokers for heart attack. But teens have a hard time understanding the risks of smoking because the onset of cancer and respiratory diseases seems very far away.

Teens are attracted to cigarettes for various reasons, even though it's against the law to target teens in advertising for cigarettes. Most try smoking because it makes them feel older or because they're trying to fit in. Teens feel that smoking gives them a sense of confidence and an outlet for stress, especially in social situations.

Sometimes, though, there may be other, more deeply psychological reasons. For example, Marcus C. began buying cigarettes when his mother was undergoing chemotherapy for lung cancer. Marcus was specifically reacting to his mother's illness by engaging in exactly the same behavior that led to his mother's illness. Marcus later realized that taking up smoking was not only ironic but destructive on his part.

Penalties for underage smoking or possession usually include fines or mandatory attendance at smoke enders or smoking awareness classes.

Trespassing, Prowling, Entering Closed Parks, and Crashing Parties

The flood control channel was a place I should have known not to enter, even if the gate was open.

Trespassing

Trespassing means an unlawful entry onto someone else's property without their permission or implied consent. Entering fenced property or property that has warning signs against entry is considered a trespass.

Jeremy T. was observed by officers with other juveniles who appeared to be involved in graffiti vandalism in the area of state property abutting a freeway. At the end of the property was a flood control channel area, which was fenced off. The officers ordered the juveniles to not move, but they all began running through the channel. Because the minors continued to elude capture, air support was called in. Jeremy was eventually taken into custody for trespassing. He was fortunate the flood control channel was not active at that time.

In another case, three girls were cited for trespassing in a fenced-off area. Even though the girls were only there to take photos for a school project and had no apparent criminal intentions, their actions were still considered a trespass.

Justin B. jumped the back fence of a secured apartment building to talk with his girlfriend, who was grounded and couldn't come out to see him. He was cited for trespassing. Anna R. was sleeping over at a friend's house when the friend had the bad idea of sneaking out of her apartment and hanging out on the roof of the building. Anna and her friend became disoriented and almost fell off the roof when police helicopters began to circle and aim their searchlights on them.

Ben D. and three friends thought they had permission from another friend to enter the backyard of an unoccupied house and go swimming. What Ben didn't know was that the house had actually been repossessed from the friend's parents and now belonged to the bank. He and his friends were cited for trespassing and Ben learned that the boarded-up house and posted signs should have deterred him from entering the backyard, notwithstanding his friend's supposed permission.

There are special trespassing laws that relate to loitering near a school campus (see, for example, section 653(b) of the California Penal Code). Even if you're a former student at the school, loitering or trespassing at a school that isn't your own can be considered an offense.

Tip

Many school campuses are closed to outsiders because of gang-related issues. Get written permission if you're visiting a friend or a former teacher at a school that's not currently your own. Even if the school is your own, you'll need permission to be in the building after regular school hours.

Prowling

The offense of **prowling** is similar to trespassing in the sense that you are on private property, loitering, wandering, or prowling, without visible or lawful business on that property with the owner or occupant. The difference is that in order to be convicted of prowling, the loitering or lingering on the property must be done with the purpose of committing a crime.

Entering Closed Parks and Crashing Parties

Parks and parklands aren't open at all hours. Make sure if you're going to spend time at a park that you know and understand its hours of operation. Most city parks display signage indicating what hours they are open. State and national parks are typically closed from sunset to sunrise. A closed, dark park is a place where you can be victimized. It's also a place where you can receive a citation.

Also, if you're crashing a party that you were not invited to—meaning you're an "unwanted" or invited guest—you could be subject to a trespassing citation.

Graffiti, Vandalism, and Possession of Vandalism Tools

The reason why I tagged was because I wanted people to see my name. It was kind of cool when I heard people saying, "Who is that?" But the week after I got busted my friend told me about a job painting a wall of a studio. His mom knew the owner. It took us two hours but we completed the wall with a beautiful art piece. This showed me I can paint legally and express myself the right way.

I tagged because I got fame on the street. I liked it when random people came up to me and told me that they'd seen my name up on a wall.

I promised my mom that if my friends ask me to write on the wall again or offer me a spray can, I would say no thanks, and I'll tell them, "Don't do it, you guys."

The night of my arrest, they found an aerosol container. I had intent to mark on a wall. But as I was walking, I decided not to because of a recent talk I had with my older brothers. I planned on just throwing the spray paint away, but before I had a chance to do that, I was caught.

Graffiti

Graffiti and other forms of vandalism are the crimes most often associated with teen perpetrators. The problem is so widespread that special undercover vandalism suppression teams often patrol city transit buses and subway systems. The problem is also so costly that many legislatures have enacted laws that prohibit not only the act of tagging itself, but also the possession of graffiti tools, that is, any items typically associated with vandalism. (See p. 108 for a list of these kinds of tools.)

Tip

There's a distinct difference between real artwork and vandalism, no matter how creative the latter is. If you're a true artist, do yourself a favor and don't carry around items that can be considered tools of vandalism. Watercolor paints, pastel chalks, and the like cannot be construed as tools used for vandalism. Spray paint, wide permanent markers (such as Sharpies), and other items that are not erasable should be left at home; don't carry them in your pockets or backpack.

Taggers often operate in groups called "crews." They are opportunistic and often vandalize while in the presence of their peers to gain status. They frequently share their tools and act as lookouts during vandalism activity. The penalties for these kinds of crimes usually include jail time, restitution, community service, and loss of driver's license for up to a year. In some jurisdictions, your parents may also be held liable for your damages.

Although much vandalism is gang-inspired and involves tagging or gang crews, not all vandalism falls into this category. Sometimes vandalism is the result of depression, anger, or other negative feelings. George M. was doing fairly well in school, but he committed vandalism while his mother was having chemo treatments for cancer. He said he did it because he needed an "outlet." Ali P. committed vandalism because his divorced parents were constantly fighting over him. Eleven-year-old Nathan punctured his teacher's tire and scratched the paint on her car after she wrote his parents a letter regarding his school performance.

> **Tip**
>
> Adopting and using a moniker—a gang nickname—although not illegal in and of itself, is a way of glorifying and associating with a gang lifestyle. Consider sticking with the name your parents gave you.

Possession of Vandal Tools and Being a Lookout for Vandalism

Graffiti tools can include spray paint cans, acrylic paints, razors, etchers, "scribes," markers, sandpaper, rocks or other sharp/hard objects, and acid.

Other common tools are "slap tags" in which taggers write graffiti on stickers, which they then use to quickly vandalize a surface with their tag crew name or moniker. Many of the tools carried by taggers can also be used as weapons.

It's also worth noting that many jurisdictions have passed laws making it a specific crime to be a "lookout" for vandalism activity.

> **Something to Think About**
>
> Vandalism is often committed on school grounds. But if you think about it, that's the place you spend a good part of your day, second only to your own home. Would you vandalize your own bathroom?

Jana S. went along with her friend as the friend tagged a girls' bathroom in school. Although Jana wasn't tagging herself, nor did she possess any of the tools used for the graffiti, she was cited for being a lookout, which essentially meant that she was aiding and abetting her friend. At court, Jana stated, "I didn't do anything. I was just there." She later understood, however, that because she was watching out and reporting to her friend as to whether school police were in the vicinity, her activities constituted being a lookout. In another case, Andres M. was cited for being a lookout because he whistled a certain tune when police officers entered an apartment building known for narcotics activity. At trial, the officer testified that lookouts often use specific whistles or tunes to alert their companions of police presence.

Tip

Search out positive outlets for depression, anger, and resentment. Ask for help from adults such as a teacher, dean, counselor, or parent, or from teen helplines. You may be more comfortable talking to a friend, but friends are often ill equipped to help solve serious problems.

Other Kinds of Vandalism

Other types of vandalism include throwing eggs or other objects at cars. Although eggs are soft and normally do not create holes or dents, the sulfur in eggs eats away at car paint, damaging it. Also, throwing any kind of object at a moving car is dangerous in that it could surprise or confuse the driver, perhaps causing him to get into an accident. If such an accident were to occur as a result of objects being thrown at the vehicle, the person throwing the object would be liable not only for the damages to the vehicle but also for any physical injuries to the driver or passengers.

In one case, Martin L. and a friend were horsing around, throwing lemons across the street. Several of the lemons hit and splattered cars, even shattering one windshield. Neighbors called the police and Martin and his friend were charged with vandalism.

John B. was an A student who often tutored a friend who was having problems in school in general and math in particular. While he was tutoring one day, the friend asked John to join him in throwing eggs at a neighbor's window. Feeling caught up in the moment, John agreed, and both John and his friend were cited for vandalism.

Ana F. used her fist to break the window in the girls' bathroom. She stated that she was mad because it wouldn't open. She was charged with vandalism.

Tip

Don't feel pressured to give a quick answer when someone asks you to do something that you know is wrong or illegal. Take a moment to think about what might happen. Don't get caught up in it. Thinking things over might give you time to talk yourself out of a bad decision.

Possession of a Knife

Ever since I bumped into a girl in the restroom, her friends would come up to me and dog me. So I called my friend and told him what happened and asked him if he could get me a knife. It was a bad idea because what if I had really gotten into a fight and lost control?

No one should carry around a knife or bring it to school. Most states have limitations on the specific size and length for legal blades, outlawing dirks, daggers, and automatic switchblades. Certain exceptions for small pocket or Swiss Army knives exist, but only under certain circumstances—for example, on a supervised camping trip.

An officer observed Ben C. sitting down on a bench near a donut shop during school hours. When Ben noticed the officer, he threw an unknown object behind a trash can, causing the officer to be suspicious. The officer retrieved the object, which turned out to be a two-and-a-half-inch locking blade. Ben claimed he had it in his pants and had forgotten to take it out. Ben was charged with possession of a knife and truancy.

Tip

If you're a camper or Boy or Girl Scout and use the same backpack for school and camping, make sure to empty the backpack of all possible illegal knives before you use the back-pack for school.

Challenging to a Fight, Fighting in School, Disturbing the Peace, and Other Related Offenses

"What are you looking at?" he said to me.
When I answered, "What are you talking about?"
he started punching me and we got into a fight.

I was going to sixth period when I see an enemy. I go up
to him and he say, "XYZ gang" and I said, "ABC gang,"
and we ended up getting down.

Fights at school or on the street often begin with seemingly innocent conversation or misunderstood looks, sometimes called "mad dogging." Other fights begin with what is commonly referred to as "trash talk" or "talking smack"—belittling friends, girlfriends, or parents. These types of incidents used to be handled at school by a school principal or dean, but they are now routinely cited to court. Sometimes the misunderstandings are cultural or language related, often ending in physical altercations with scratches, bruises, and bleeding. Besides a citation to court, they usually lead to a suspension or an expulsion from school.

Arthur C. started a fight with a classmate who was sending annoying text messages to a friend's sister. Roman L. became involved in a fight at school that related to one group of kids wanting the air conditioner on while another group of kids wanted it off. Elena M. became involved in a fight with another girl based on a misunderstanding about a borrowed iPod. The person who borrowed her iPod claimed another girl had taken it, and then the borrower retaliated by taking the girl's camera.

Tip

Don't bring expensive items such as iPods, cameras, and other electronic gadgets to school. They're easily lost or stolen, and may become the subject of misunderstandings and fights.

Manuel B. started a fight because someone had been talking disrespectfully about his mom. The verbal assault escalated into pushing and shoving, which then escalated again into exchanging punches. Manuel and his companion didn't stop even after being yelled at by security, and pepper spray was then used by the officers. In the end, both students were taken to the hospital with swelling, redness, pain, and chemical burns from the pepper spray.

"Bothering" and bullying—whether verbal or physical—goes on in some degree in every school. Ethan M. got so fed up with a schoolmate's bullying him that he threw the schoolmate's shoes in the toilet. In an instant, he went from victim to perpetrator, and was cited to court for vandalism.

Sometimes there are racial- or ethnic-group–related components to school fights. Different cultural cues or behaviors are often misunderstood, leading to fights. Offenses motivated by hatred or dislike for others may be classified as hate crimes, a more serious offense. A hate crime is an offense committed against a person (or the person's property) because of certain perceived or real characteristics about the person. These include the person's race, ethnicity, religion, ancestry, national origin, disability, gender, or sexual orientation. In some cases, threats and intimidation can also be enough to constitute a hate crime. Although words alone—such as using an ethnic or racial slur—aren't a crime, if the words can be construed as a threat of violence against a specific person or group, the words aren't protected under the First Amendment of the Constitution.

Finally, even among good friends, misunderstandings can happen. Pamela K. and Leanne G. were best friends for five years and often slept over at each other's houses. One night, Leanne thought Pamela had stolen twenty dollars out of her purse. Even though the twenty-dollar bill was found on the floor, Leanne continued to blame Pamela, and their disagreement spilled over to school the next day. They fought each other at school, and their five-year friendship ended based on one unfortunate incident.

Tip

Try to manage your frustration and anger—even if it is justifiable—and walk away from situations. Report bullying to the proper authorities. Even if it wasn't you who threw the first punch, if you continue a fight, you become responsible for it. It's usually very difficult to determine who started the fight and/or to prove self-defense with regard to a fight at school.

A challenge or encouragement to fight can also be construed as an offense. When there's a high level of tension between certain racial groups, school officials often impose and enforce a zero-tolerance policy. James B. was observed instigating an altercation between a Hispanic group and an African American group by shouting and making threatening gestures. Although he didn't touch or hit anyone, he was cited for disturbing the peace.

Loud music, rowdiness, partying at a very late hour, and attending a party where there's drug or alcohol use can also be considered **disturbing the peace**. Also, if you disrupt a professional sporting event by

Tip

Don't be a rubbernecker—if you see something going down in school or on the street, don't walk toward the commotion, walk away from it. Don't let other people egg you on to a fight.

throwing something onto the field or distract a player or interfere in any way with the event, you may be subject to a fine.

Shoplifting and Other Petty Thefts

I never thought I would be here in court. I'm not a thief in any way, shape, or form. And I'm nothing but an honest person. I just had a roadblock.

I shoplifted at Macy's. I'm still not sure why I did it. Maybe it was because I wanted to prove to my so-called friend that I was "down" to do it.

I don't have the need to be stealing. The reason why I did it is because I thought it was easy to go inside the store, steal a couple of CDs, and get some money for them.

What happens to you when you're caught? Well, you go to a room where you are sat down and told to empty everything you took. Then you're given a chance to call your parents. If no one answers they call the police, and if your parents still don't come, you go to jail.

Shoplifting

Teens shoplift for various reasons. Sometimes it's about wanting attention from distracted parents, wanting to push the envelope, wanting to see how it feels, or wanting to impress friends. Other times, it might be a matter of impulse. Make sure you know who your friends really are, and how they are likely to behave. If they've told you that they've shoplifted on previous occasions, avoid going shopping with them.

When I asked Dana T. why she shoplifted from an electronics store, she answered, "Because I thought I could get away with it." Dana didn't stop to consider that an electronics store, of all places, would have the best in electronic video surveillance.

The afternoon before her homecoming dance, Mona N. impulsively shoplifted $200 worth of jewelry to wear that night. She was detained by police and wasn't able to attend the dance. Although the dance and what she wore was important to her before the incident, afterward Mona realized how unimportant they were. She described her detention by store employees as "life-altering," something that made her want to improve her life and get better grades.

Jarrod S. had an older cousin who was disabled. Jarrod accompanied his cousin to K-Mart, pushing his cousin's wheelchair. Because his disabled cousin couldn't reach up toward the top shelf, he asked Jarrod to take down a DVD, which Jarrod did. To Jarrod's surprise, his cousin proceeded to open up the DVD case and take out the DVD, and then asked Jarrod to put the empty DVD case back on the shelf. At court Jarrod maintained that he didn't know of his cousin's intentions to steal when they entered the store, but the moment he understood, he shouldn't have continued to be involved in the cousin's theft. Jarrod was cited for shoplifting along with his cousin.

Shoplifting hurts not only you and your parents, but your community as well. Even stores owned by large companies are victims of your theft. Stores don't absorb the cost of shoplifting—they pass along their increased costs for security and surveillance to other consumers in the form of higher prices.

Keep in mind, too, that most states entitle merchants to assess a civil fine (sometimes called a **notice of civil demand**) against you or your parents if you are caught shoplifting. This fine is in addition to any criminal penalties or fines that may be imposed as part

Something to Think About

Is it fair to the people in your community—your parents included—to have to pay more for the items they buy in a store because you and others have shoplifted?

of the criminal prosecution process. You and your parents may also have to sign a juvenile criminal trespass warning whereby you promise not to enter or remain on any premises belonging to the store at which you shoplifted without parental supervision for a period of time, often up to two years. If you violate the agreement, you might be prosecuted for criminal trespass.

Showing that you didn't intend to steal isn't always easy to prove. Barbara W. went to the mall for the afternoon with friends. In one store, Barbara tried on hats, scarves, and jewelry. She put most of the merchandise back, but left the store while still wearing one of the rings she'd tried on. When cited for shoplifting, she claimed she had no intent to steal but rather was distracted by her friends and didn't realize she was still wearing one of the items she'd tried on.

Teen theft most often occurs around birthdays, holidays, and Valentine's Day. These are times where there's pressure to buy gifts for someone you care about. Remember, though, that anyone who truly

Tip

If you walk into a store with a friend or family member and she begins stealing, best thing you can do is to turn around and put distance between yourself and your friend or relative. Even if you're not the one stealing, you're bound to get into the same trouble as she does, just by being in proximity to her.

Tip

When you're in a store and just trying things on, make sure you keep the merchandise visible. Be aware of your obligation to return all merchandise to its proper place. Don't get distracted by friends or phone calls and leave with merchandise on your person. Be aware of store parameters. Don't step out of a store with merchandise to chat with your friends who are outside the store.

cares for you—your boyfriend, your sister, or your mother—would rather have no gift from you than have a gift that has been shoplifted. Finally, consider that shoplifting a $1.89 bag of candy is still a misdemeanor, something you might have to disclose on a college or employment application one day. Many employers don't want to take a chance on hiring a shoplifter—even a former, one-time shoplifter.

Tip

What may start out as a prank may end up as a citation for theft. Most pranks rarely end well.

Other Thefts

Theft also occurs at school, such as theft of school equipment, cell phones, backpacks, money, sodas, and even baseball hats. Sometimes the theft starts out as a prank. Scott L. thought it would be funny to take twenty dollars out of Diane M.'s purse. He considered it only a "prank" and intended to return the money. Other people got involved, however, sending the victim text messages naming Scott, and the victim reported the theft to her school police. Scott was cited for a petty theft. Nathan E. stole money from a fund-raising bake sale at school. Not only was he prosecuted for theft, but his popularity at school suffered as well.

Sixteen-year-old Elvin R. saw a stack of bottled drinks sitting on a neighbor's front porch and decided to steal the drinks. He brought his thirteen-year-old brother along to help him haul it away and both were cited for theft.

Keeping Lost Property and Receiving Stolen Property

Keeping Lost Property

If you find lost property under circumstances that give you the knowledge of or means to inquire about the property's owner, and instead take it for your own use without making reasonable efforts to locate the owner, you're guilty of theft. If you find someone's wallet, for example, with a license and address inside, and you don't make any attempt to contact the owner or hand it over to a police station, you may be liable for the offense of keeping lost property. If, on the other hand, you find a dollar bill on the street, with no identifying marks on the bill or way to find the owner, you would not be liable for keeping lost property.

Tip

If you find something valuable at school, don't put it in your pocket or your backpack and wait until later to find out who it belongs to. It's better to hand the item over immediately to a teacher, a dean, or the school office. Even if you plan to return the property later, keeping the item may be construed as an intention on your part not to return it to its rightful owner.

Receiving Stolen Property

Even if you didn't steal the property, you can be prosecuted for buying a stolen item. To be guilty of this crime, you must know that it was stolen—but such knowledge can be proven by circumstantial evidence, meaning evidence that's inferred from other sources. Circumstantial evidence could include, for example, that you paid much less for an item compared to what the item usually cost in a store, that there was an attempt to hide the item, or that identifying marks (such as serial numbers) had been removed from the item.

Tip

Don't buy things off the street from people you don't know. If the price is too good to be true, it is likely the item is stolen or pirated.

Fare Evasion

Fare evasion means not paying the correct fare—or failing to pay any fare at all—on a city bus or subway. Examples might include using the back door to enter a bus without paying or jumping over a turnstile to avoid payment; it's also considered fare evasion if you use someone else's bus pass or monthly stickers, or use fake or forged bus or subway passes. Similar to fare evasion is defrauding a ski resort by not paying for your lift tickets, or sneaking into a movie theater, arcade, or an amusement park.

Setting Fires, Illegal Campfires, Fire Alarms, and Fireworks

Setting off a fire alarm when there is no fire is wrong for a number of reasons. First of all, it's a waste of the firefighters' time. They could be going to a real fire. Also people could get hurt trying to avoid what they think is a fire. People might panic.

Depending on the circumstances and the amount of damages, setting a fire can be either a misdemeanor or a felony. Setting off a fire alarm at school or other public location is also considered a misdemeanor in most jurisdictions. An alarm at school wastes time and valuable resources of local law enforcement and the fire department, and it also creates a disturbance at school by forcing an evacuation.

Similarly, bringing firecrackers or any other incendiary material to school can also be a misdemeanor. Substances and items that aren't easily identified on the scene may have to be disposed of by a bomb squad, causing further expenditure of time and money.

Marlin S. was fooling around with matches to ignite nail polish remover on the sidewalk outside of school. Although there was little damage from the incident, he was cited for setting a fire.

Twelve-year-old Bonnie R. and her friends decided to bring matchbooks to school. They tore up pieces of paper and started a small fire at the back of the schoolyard. Although there was no actual property damage, the potential for damage on a hot, dry, windy day was enormous. Bonnie was charged with setting unlawful fires. When asked why she had lit the paper on fire, she replied, "I have no idea."

Illegal Street Sales

Selling merchandise on the street requires a sales permit. Marvin B. was trying to be entrepreneurial by selling original CDs produced by a local band. He thought that because the music was original and he was not selling illegal knock-offs, he could promote the band by selling the CDs at certain locations. Unfortunately, he didn't realize he needed to acquire a proper permit or license to sell on the street.

Offenses Relating to Computers and the Internet

Most states have laws that prohibit pirating or downloading copyrighted material such as music; accessing someone else's computer without authorization; deleting, damaging, or destroying systems, networks, programs, databases, or components of computers without authorization; disrupting access to authorized users of a computer; and introducing viruses to a computer. New laws are being enacted every day regarding legal and illegal uses of computers and the Internet.

CHAPTER 7

What Can I Expect at Court?

When I first walked out of the courtroom, I thought to myself that my punishment wasn't fair. Now I realize just how fair it was.

Before attending the classes I was assigned, I was filled with a feeling of reluctance. I did not see the reason as to why I had to attend the class. I just did it to get my hours done. The day before I remember complaining to my friends about the punishments I received, and they were all very sympathetic. The next day I went to the class, and I was surprised to hear the things I heard.

The disposition of your case and subsequent orders will be based on and tailored to your particular offense. Some dispositions are mandated by law (also called **mandatory sentencing**). Mostly though, a juvenile court judge will have wide **discretion** in making orders. Mitigating circumstances; your school, mental health, and social history; specific needs; and prior offenses will also be taken into account, as well as the ability and willingness of your parents to help you comply with the court's orders. This is all in keeping with the philosophical mandate of the juvenile court system—to rehabilitate minors rather than punish them, as discussed in chapter 1.

Priors

The judge will have a copy of your record—your **priors** and their dispositions. When determining what orders to make, the judge will take in to account whether this is your first offense, or whether you've already committed this particular offense or others previously. A second speeding ticket, for example, is more serious than the first, and a third more serious than the second. So, too, a second shoplifting offense will be handled more severely than a first-time shoplifting. The judge will expect you to have learned from your mistakes and if it seems you have not, your penalty will be more rigorous.

Different Kinds of Dispositions/Orders

I know my mom is tired of coming to court and paying for my problems. She needs it to pay the bills and stuff for my sister, and we need to pay the people we owe money to.

License Suspensions/Revocations/Restrictions

The past sixty days have been horrible. The use of public transportation and walking should be only a last resort and have given me a new appreciation of my much-missed driver's license.

A *license suspension* means you cannot drive under any circumstances. Sometimes the court will physically confiscate your license and you will have to return to court to pick it up after the suspension period.

A *license restriction* means you may retain possession of your license and you may drive, but only under certain conditions. Typically, the court might allow you to drive (1) to and from your job,

(2) during the course of your job, (3) to and from a treatment program, and (4) to and from school. The court may allow you to drive under any one of these conditions, or a combination. Another type of restriction allows you to drive, but only with a parent or licensed driver over the age of twenty-five in a position to instruct you in the car.

Tip

The more you show the judge that you want to take responsibility for your actions, rather than expecting your parents or someone else to, the more mature and trustworthy you appear to the court.

A *license revocation* means that before you can resume driving you must apply for a new license and may be retested. The severity of your offense, mandatory sentencing with regard to certain offenses, and/or past offenses will dictate which intervention will be applied.

Fines

The judge must follow penalty or bail guidelines imposed by law or local rules. Generally, though, he has a certain degree of discretion with regard to fines.

A fine is usually made up of the **fine** itself, a **penalty assessment,** which is an additional amount added to all fines on infractions and low-grade misdemeanors, and which may be 200 percent in addition to the fine, along with other surcharges and fees, such as a traffic school violator fee. If you look up your offense in the code books, the fines listed may not include the penalty assessments and other surcharges levied by local governments.

The judge will not be addressing your parents when she asks you if you're paying the fine. He'll be addressing you! Don't look to your parents for the answer when this question is asked.

If a fine is imposed and you can't pay on your court date, you can request an extension to pay, but expect a late fee to be added to your fine.

Traffic School

I thought traffic school would be a total waste of time.
Then they showed us a movie about teens who died in
a car accident, and it showed all the gory details.
Those were four lives lost for no reason at all.

Traffic school attendance is discretionary on the part of the judge hearing your case. Its benefits are twofold: (1) It reviews rules of the road, and (2) it removes the offense (or point) from your department of motor vehicles record. It also removes the offense for the purposes of insurance. Insurance companies charge high premiums to insure minors, and a point on your record normally raises your insurance premium.

Tip

Plan ahead and take responsibility. Your parents shouldn't have to pay for an offense they did not commit. If you know you're most likely going to be assessed a fine, discuss this with your parents and make a plan. If you're not working and your parents agree to pay for your fine, commit to reimbursing them. Make a payment plan or pledge to do extra chores at home. If your parents require you to pay them back for fines they've paid on your behalf, that is good parenting on their part.

Most states have rules regarding how often you can attend traffic school. In California, for example, you may attend traffic school only once every eighteen months. The eighteen-month time period is calculated from citation date to citation date, not from the time you attended your last traffic school class.

Traffic school is usually an eight-hour class. Some jurisdictions also allow a twelve-hour second-chance traffic school for a second offense committed during an eighteen-month period, which has to be requested and allowed by a judge.

Many traffic schools are now available online, but make sure your local rules allow you to participate in such a class. Some jurisdictions don't allow online traffic school for minors.

Improvement in School

I faked my progress report because I did not have enough time to get all my teacher's signatures. That was a big mistake. I feel very stupid now to have done that.

Improvement in school is an indicator of your willingness and commitment to make a positive change in your life. This improvement—pulling up your grades, attending all classes, and not being tardy, ditching, or suspended—is an important component in most court orders. If your court orders include improvement in school along with community service, completing the community service alone won't put you in compliance with your orders. School attendance and marked improvement is essential to rehabilitation.

Community Service

I did community service at a Korean health and education center. Here, I had a chance to meet a lot of poor people who need great help. I felt that I am so fortunate to be born in a financially stable and comfortable family that I don't have to worry about bare necessities of life. For example, I am driving a brand new Honda Accord that my parents bought for me. Until now I took it for granted because all my friends are in a similar situation. But now I am aware that there are people who cannot get the least that they are supposed to have.

I worked at an animal shelter, cleaning out cages and did lots of feeding and watering. I was also able to help by loading fifty-pound bags of pet food onto a truck. This was a big help because the women and a lot of kids were not able to lift the heavy bags.

I worked at a thrift store called Out of the Closet. This was very different for me because all the employees were either gay or lesbian. I learned something from all of them. They're just the same as everyone else.

During my last week of working at the retirement hotel, one of the residents passed away suddenly. The only people who seemed to notice were the volunteers and the employees. His family did not show up to claim his belongings for almost a week after his death. I discovered that it is not the illnesses or exhaustion that brings about the death of the residents. Their deaths are prompted by the loneliness of the retirement home.

I didn't enjoy the community service (not that I was supposed to) because I got blisters all over my hands, I got allergies and I couldn't see or breathe because of all the dirt, and I had to get up at 5:00 a.m. when I didn't have to.

Community service covers a wide variety of volunteer jobs that benefit the community at large. It is also designed to instill a sense of responsibility. Most people think of community service as only graffiti cleanup and picking up trash on streets. But community service can also include jobs such as repairing wheelchairs; sorting cans and food at a food bank; clerical and filing, fund-raising, maintenance, and yard work at a school or recreation center; helping at a public library, old age home, or hospital; organizing and collecting clothes for the homeless; and taking part in pet adoption and animal services at an animal shelter. All these are vital community interests that can also build life and job skills that might help you later on when you enter the job market.

Your parents will most likely have to sign authorizations for permission to participate in community service along with an authorization for emergency medical care and a release from liability.

Drug and Alcohol Classes

Drug and alcohol classes examine emotional and physical factors related to drug abuse, such as mood, expectation, previous experiences, weight, sex, health, and factors such as setting and whether drugs are used with friends, with strangers, or alone. They sometimes also cover the history of psychoactive drugs, and the differences between stimulants (such as amphetamines), depressants, and psychedelics. Class discussions include the importance of exercise, alternatives, individual vulnerability to stress, relaxation techniques, time management skills, and how to approach and solve daily problems. Chemical dependency education classes also cover topics such as the consequences of drug and alcohol abuse, denial, the importance of honesty and changing friends, understanding why people use drugs, and learning how to deal with triggers and cravings.

Smoking Awareness Classes

If you've been cited for possession of tobacco or tobacco paraphernalia, you might be sent to a smoking awareness class. These classes cover the obvious dangers of tobacco, including various types of cancer, emphysema, bronchitis, and heart attack, along with other, less obvious dangers, such as alcohol interaction, allergies, cavities, fetal smoking syndrome, bad breath, headaches, infertility, and wrinkles.

Classes explore individual personal history, chemical compounds contained in tobacco, dependency, tips for quitting, stress triggers, and the financial costs of maintaining a cigarette habit.

Drug Testing

If you're ordered to undergo periodic drug testing, the court will normally refer you to an authorized lab. Home drug-testing kits are not usually acceptable in court. Most drug-testing labs screen for the following drugs: amphetamines, barbiturates, cocaine, methadone, methamphetamine (Ecstasy), opiates, phencyclidine (PCP), THC (cannabis and marijuana), and tricyclic antidepressants (TCA). They may also test for benzodiazepine, buprenorphine (Subutex), oxycodone, and EDDP.

There are unreliable Web sites that sell products that claim to "beat" drug tests. Don't be fooled by these claims. Reputable labs are aware of all possible neutralizing or masking agents. Don't try to adulterate test samples by drinking excessive amounts of water or flushing products. A low creatinine level may be considered evidence of flushing.

Let the lab know if you're taking any over-the-counter drugs, such as cough medication, any mood-altering drugs (benzodiazepines) such as Valium or Xanax, or drugs such as Vicodin, Tylenol 3, Percocet, Darvocet, or any other opiates that might interfere with the drug test.

Also, don't ask someone else to take the drug test for you or bring another person's urine samples with you to a drug test. These methodologies are well known, and treatment centers test for other factors you might not be aware of, such as temperature of the urine.

Long-Term Rehabilitation or "Rehab"

You've probably heard about "rehab" in movies, television, and even pop/rock songs. Rehab, otherwise known as **rehabilitation facilities**, come in all shapes and forms. Sometimes the court will order you or refer you to a specific treatment facility; other times the court might allow you and your parents to choose a treatment facility, as long as the court is satisfied that the facility is reputable and effective.

Orders for long-term rehabilitation are usually made in cases where there's been a history of substance abuse and other legal proceedings along with a history of school suspensions, truancy, or failure at school. Long-term treatment programs last anywhere from two to twelve months. Others may work with clients on an outpatient basis, requiring consistent attendance and effort in weekly group and/or individual counseling sessions.

Long-term rehabilitation facilities stress the importance of following rules, respect for staff, and interaction with other residents. Treatment focuses on coping skills, social skills, delay of gratification, anger management, and improvement in family relationships through family therapy.

After successfully completing a formal rehab setting, the court may also order you to continue with a twelve-step program such as

Alcoholics Anonymous or Marijuana Anonymous on a regular basis.

Essays

As I was reading the story about a very bad car accident, I pictured myself as the teen being described.

The short story was about a seventeen-year-old boy who was killed in a car accident. The point was if someone was to be killed in such a way it would impact not only that person, but also their family and their friends. Even if I didn't die right away, and I was sitting in a hospital bed knowing I was going to die and seeing my mom and my sister and all my friends and my girlfriend crying next to me would just be way too much for me to handle.

Writing this essay, I find myself thinking different thoughts and in a logical light.

The judge might assign you to write an essay as a response to a reading assignment, topics related to your offense, questions about your future plans, or a daily journal. Writing an essay is not just busywork, but a way of engaging you in a dialogue with the court and with yourself. Some teens are able to organize their thoughts better in writing, clarifying feelings they aren't able to talk about. This helps put your offense in perspective and set goals in writing.

Therapy and Counseling

I think that the best experience of them all was going to the counselor. I had many internal conflicts and many conflicts in my family that I had always kept bottled up. Once I went to the psychiatrist he made me write my feelings and thoughts and many other things. This was really good because I got to see what really bothered me and where everything was coming from.

I suppose I'm angry because I grew up without a man in my family.

Everyone has heard the expression "acting out" with regard to teenagers. Teens acting out of resentment and crying for attention often end up in court. Even though there's a great deal of awareness of the therapeutic benefits of psychotherapy, many teens still believe that therapy isn't for them, that they "don't need it," or there must be something wrong with them if they're ordered to go to therapy. If you're so ordered into therapy, don't immediately discount it—give it a chance. Although there are no magic bullets in therapy, a process that might take weeks or months, you might actually enjoy talking things out with a neutral person, someone who's not a friend or family member.

Yolany F. was very unhappy about her parents' divorce, and she blamed her mother for instigating it. Living with her mother, Yolany refused to follow rules, ditched school, and even assaulted her mother on one occasion. Family therapy helped her understand that she was repeating patterns of domestic violence she had witnessed at home with her father.

Ellen T. began using drugs at a young age. After a while, drugs weren't enough and she began to self-mutilate. Therapy brought out the resentment Ellen felt because she hardly ever saw her mother, who was incarcerated for drugs in state prison.

Evan R. threw a chair at a school dean because the dean allegedly gestured the letter "L" (for "loser") with his index finger and thumb. Therapy helped him understand that his lack of friends at school and feelings of inferiority were the basis for his out-of-control behavior.

Emily N. was taken from her home by the state and was living with her aunt when she was caught shoplifting. Therapy helped her sort out her feelings about her mother and father, who had committed a burglary while her three-month-old sibling was left in the car. Both parents had engaged in drug abuse, physical abuse, and domestic violence, and a court had terminated Emily's father's parental rights.

Rona B.'s grades were dropping and she was having problems with her mother, which led to her taking the car out and driving without a license. The source of the conflict was later identified in therapy—Rona had been raped a year before and had refused to make a police report, something her mother had strongly advised. Her inability to deal with or talk about the rape had been the catalyst behind her acting out.

Hospital Programs

I was assigned to go to a program at the emergency room and while I was sitting there until 1:00 a.m., I was thinking that I was lucky that I am ordered to go through all these so that I learn a lesson before I actually end up in the emergency room as a patient.

Though the class did teach me things I never knew, I feel it did not apply to me and my own life. It was not necessary for the violation that I received.

Hospital programs are designed to give teens a glimpse into the fragility of life. Spending an evening at a local emergency room is very different from watching *ER* on television. Teens see real people with real life-and-death issues. It helps them appreciate their own lives and their good health.

Morgue Programs

When I was assigned to go to the hospital and morgue, I immediately felt uneasy and nervous. The morgue was less of a waste of my time. I got to walk with death and the result was a greater appreciation of life. I saw the cold fragile bodies of people that used to breathe like I do now. It could happen to anyone at any time.

After the slides, we put on shoe coverings, face masks, and gloves and all proceeded down into the "meat locker." There were 344 bodies. It was 45 degrees down there and smelled terribly. I looked right back into the stare of death.

At first when I was told to do this program, I thought, Wow what a stupid way of trying to help someone. *All it's going to do is gross them out and make them have bad dreams, but it does so much more than that.*

Morgue programs are usually assigned to teens who have committed drug and alcohol offenses or other offenses considered dangerous and reckless. Morgue programs are scary eye-openers, as they incorporate all your senses, including sight, smell, and cold. Parents may be required to accompany their teens to the program, which is run by the local county coroner's office. Participating teens usually wear special clothing and protective gear.

Tolerance Programs

I was assigned an assignment to go to the Museum of Tolerance, which is located in Los Angeles. Well at first I thought that this would be boring, but when I got there it actually was fun and I learned a lot. We have these problems these days in our own life. You see people fighting because they are not the same race or religion. I myself consider it wrong because after all we all are just human.

In learning many facts about the Holocaust, I felt very bad for what happened to those innocent people. I have to admit that I have been racist at some times and that I have shown prejudice to some, but I also believe there is not one person who has never done that.

Teens involved in school fights, vandalism, and other offenses that involve racial bias are sometimes sent, along with other appropriate orders, to museums or activities that promote tolerance. Los Angeles, for example, has a Museum of Tolerance, and New York has a Tolerance Center.

These programs are specifically intended to inspire students to learn from the past and engage with others who are different from them. They also facilitate dialogue, private journaling, and group-sharing reflection, providing ground rules for open and respectful dialogue and hoping to make a positive difference in fighting prejudice and hate. Some programs offer interactive high-tech experiences; others may simply engage teens in useful discourse, opening up new channels of communication.

Stress and Anger Management Programs

Stress and anger management programs explore the causes of anger and the triggers that make people feel angry, such as helplessness, loneliness, feeling stupid, and feeling people aren't paying attention to you. They also help you understand how men and women express anger in different ways.

These programs also have you participate in exercises to help you express your emotions, including role playing ways to deal with outbursts and cope with criticism, channeling rather than repressing anger, unhealthy manipulations, positive affirmations, and discovering healthy ways of expressing anger. Other exercises can include breathing techniques, word repetition, using imagery for relaxation, and nonstrenuous exercise such as yoga to relax muscles and help calm you down.

Straight Talk, Diversion, and Behavior Modification Programs

At the end of the program they had the group write a letter called "A Letter from an Angel." The letter gave us all a chance to say goodbye to the loved ones who would be most affected by us dying. I wasn't sure how to take this at first. I was scared to show my true feelings.

Some diversion programs are funded by federal grants; others, by your local school district or police. There are also programs overseen by volunteer centers, assistance leagues, and private, for-profit programs.

These programs usually discuss topics such as self-esteem, anger management, stress management, coping skills, effective communication, conflict resolution, goal setting, and taking responsibility for one's actions. They might also talk about the underlying reasons for substance abuse, such as depression, anger, grief, trauma, and resentment.

The programs sometimes ask you to share your personal story with the group and to write down your answers to questions in a program workbook. You might be asked how you feel about the incident, the amount of money the incident cost you and your family, and any insight you've gained from the experience. You might also be given handouts with information regarding the laws that apply to your situation.

In "Straight Talk" programs, also known as "Scared Straight" or boot camp–style weekend programs, the courses are more regimented. You will be expected to conform to a behavior and dress code similar to an army training camp—shirts tucked in, no sagging pants, no jewelry of any kind, no makeup, shoes tied, no sunglasses or hoods, etc.—and to adhere to strict rules. You will address all officers and other adults by "Sir" or "Ma'am" and you must request permission to speak. You will also participate in rigorous physical activity such as running, jumping jacks, sit-ups, push-ups, and so on. Your parents will also be required to attend parenting classes.

The Juvenile Probation and Court Services Department of Cook County, Chicago, has developed innovative pre- and postadjudication programs in an effort to hold juvenile offenders accountable for their conduct while at the same time helping to develop positive life skills. These programs include Victim Impact Panels for Minors, Violence Intervention Programs, Evening Reporting Centers, Employment Programs, Project Dance, Art Therapy Programs, and Animal Assisted Therapy Programs.

Parenting Classes

I'm going to be a daddy and I'm leaving all of this behind so I'm actually working in construction and trying to get some money and prepare myself to be a good dad and I don't want my baby growing up knowing his or her dad used to be from a gang.

Parenting Classes for You

Teenage parents are usually assigned a social worker, whether or not they are involved in the juvenile court system, to help guide them through the pregnancy and parenting process. Parenting classes are designed to help teen parents cope with the additional stress of parenting at such a young age.

Sixteen-year-old Crystal G. was charged with driving without a license for a second time. Crystal ran out of diapers for her one-year-old child, and drove in order to purchase them. Driving without a license not only endangered her and the other people on the road, it also endangered her own child. Her orders included not only community service and attendance and improvement in school, but also parenting classes, which, among other things, taught her better planning with regard to supplies she needed for her baby.

Parenting Classes for Your Parents

In some jurisdictions, parenting classes may be ordered for your parents along with your own orders. Most parenting classes review parenting methods and choices, developing values, consequences and individuality, teaching good association skills, rules, rewards and penalties, communication, and goal setting for the family. Exploratory questions such as "How many times have you completed your child's chores?" and "How many times did you feel guilty for yelling at your child?" might also be discussed.

Restitution

Restitution is an order made by the court for the minor to pay a sum of money to compensate a victim for the monetary costs of a crime, usually involving property damage. Restitution may be paid in one lump sum or over time, according to an agreement between the victim and perpetrator.

"Stay Away" or "Don't Associate" Orders

A "stay away" order is an order issued by the court that prohibits a person from meeting another person or contacting her by any mode of communication, including letter, e-mail, phone, text message, or instant messaging. These orders are usually appropriate when there has been some kind of harassment or unwanted attention or communication between two people.

Brandon E. and his friends were upset with Josh L. for an incident that occurred in school and decided to throw foodstuffs all over Josh's parents' driveway. Even though it was only food, it damaged the driveway. Brandon and his friends were ordered to pay restitution, were put on probation, and were ordered to stay away from Josh. Although they mostly complied, they were photographed at a party Josh attended. For their failure to comply with the "stay away" order, they served three days in juvenile hall.

Other "stay away" or "do not contact" orders may require you to stay away from victims or witnesses relating to the offense that was charged against you.

"Don't associate" orders are typical probation orders prohibiting a person on probation from associating with known felons, those engaged in any behavior that constitutes a violation of criminal law, those known by the probationer to be narcotic or drug users, or any other persons and places identified by probation. The orders might also include not associating with known gang members.

Order Not to Leave the City, County, or State

You may be required to enter into an agreement between you and the court to not leave the city, county, or state without specific court approval. It may be part of your conditions of probation.

Warrantless Search

Another typical condition of probation may be that you submit your person, residence, or any property under your control to search and seizure at any time of the day or night by a law enforcement officer, with or without a warrant.

Progressive Sanctions

Progressive sanctions are orders that become progressively more intrusive and rigorous if you continue to fail to comply with court orders.

Home Confinement and Electronic Monitoring

Minors are sometimes released from custody under a judicial order of home confinement. The confinement includes supervision from a probation officer, including evening, weekend, and holiday visitation. Electronic monitoring can be ordered by the court as an alternative to secure detention for nonviolent minors who have violated probation, home confinement, or other orders. Participants wear monitoring bracelets electronically linked to a transmitter/receiver that immediately alerts the probation officer if the minor leaves his home.

Formal Probation

Probation is a legal status imposed by a judge. A minor on probation is allowed to remain in the community under certain specific conditions that require lawful behavior, education, restitution, community service, and other treatment plans. A violation of probation may initiate new proceedings leading to incarceration.

Placements and Incarceration

Suitable Placement

Under some circumstances, a minor must be removed from his home to reside in a suitable placement facility that best addresses his needs. Placements are ordered where the court believes the minor would best benefit from an environment more restrictive than home or in cases where the parents are not able to exert sufficient discipline over the minor.

The placements can be out-of-home care ranging from group homes and psychiatric hospitals to foster care with relatives or nonrelatives. Placement decisions are made depending upon the appropriate type of setting necessary to maximize the services to be provided and to ease the transition back into his or her home and community.

Juvenile Hall

Juvenile halls are short-term detention facilities for juveniles, similar to county jails for adults. Los Angeles County, for example, has three juvenile hall facilities—Sylmar Juvenile Hall, Los Padrinos Juvenile Hall, and Eastlake Juvenile Hall. These halls are located in both urban and industrial areas, and are completely enclosed by fences topped with razor wire. The halls are equipped with surveillance cameras and staffed with probation officers and guards. Visiting hours are very limited (Saturdays and Sundays only) and only parents are allowed, except in cases where special permission has been granted by the probation department. All visitors are screened for weapons and drugs, and must adhere to a strict dress code.

In New York, juvenile detention facilities are under the supervision of the Department of Juvenile Justice (DJJ). In secure facilities like Horizon, Crossroads and Bridges Juvenile Centers, movement is restricted by physical door locks, and residents must be accompanied by staff at all times. In nonsecure facilities such as Beach Avenue and St. Germaine's Lincoln Hall, residents have more freedom of movement. In both types of facilities, residents are regularly searched for contraband.

Boot Camps

Boot camps provide long-term intensive intervention in a residential setting. These are not the same as the "boot camp-style" weekend programs discussed above. These are secured, fenced-in camps that provide structured work experience, vocational training, tutoring, and athletic activities and provide an intermediate sanction between probation and incarceration in state prisons. Some specialized camps train minors in wild land fire suppression, while others train minors in forestry. In Los Angeles, for example, the Probation Department runs nineteen boot camps with the capacity to house 2,125 minors. The average length of camp programs is 23.8 weeks.

Prison/Youth Authority

Prison is the most severe form of detention for youths and is equivalent to a state prison sentence for adults. It is not a likely sentence for the offenses listed in this guide. It is worth understanding, however, that prisons for juveniles are not that much different from prisons for adults. Housing in prison includes both dormitories and cells. High-risk wards may be escorted to showers and toilets, and sex offenders are segregated in special sex offender units.

CHAPTER 8

Returning to Court, the DMV, and Will I Have a Record?

What I want is to grow up and study something good. I also want to be a good influence for my little sister. I want her to be better than me when she grows up.

Your return to court and compliance with all court orders signifies not only an end to your court case, but also your success in making some important changes in your life. I've witnessed significant improvements and turnarounds in juvenile offenders, not only with regard to grades and attendance but also in their relationships with their parents. Compliance is something the court recognizes as an accomplishment on your part. Living up to the orders of the court shows your ability to set goals and follow guidelines, something that will hopefully help you in your future, noncourt endeavors.

Compliance

Compliance means you've obeyed all the orders of the court but does not mean your citation has been dismissed. Make sure you return your paperwork to court on time and complete all orders. Don't expect the court to give you compliance on an order or a reduction of your fine if you've only completed 75 percent of your orders. The court will expect you to comply 100 percent.

School Attendance

School attendance may count heavily. If you complete all your community service but are still truant or tardy or failing classes, the court may not consider this to be compliance with its orders.

Requesting Extensions

The court will usually give you a reasonable amount of time to complete your orders and will expect you to complete them by the date indicated. Courts differ on the granting of extensions. If your paperwork indicates "No Extensions Granted," the court probably means what it says. If, however, you have a legitimate and reasonable reason for not complying with the court's order, for example, a medical reason or death in the family, tell the court and be sure to back up your claim and request for extension with documentation of your illness, disability, or hospital stay.

Probation Report

If you've been placed on formal probation, your assigned probation officer will present a report to the judge on how you're doing. The report includes your attendance and grades during the probationary period, drug test results, and any violations of probation. The report also includes a recommendation to the judge. Below is an example of language typically found in a probation officer's report:

> On 8/27/07, the court deemed the progress report a violation of minor's probation and informed the minor that should he continue to violate his conditions of probation he would be ordered to complete a six-month boot camp program. Minor had numerous absences in all six classes and was issued another citation for being in possession of alcohol. It is

respectfully recommended that the home on probation order dated 1/05/07 be terminated and a new order of removal from the community be granted.

Falsifying Documents

I faked my progress report because I did not have enough time to get all my teachers' signatures. The reason why was because I just had remembered yesterday after school that I had court the next day. By the time I was able to get my attendance, all my teachers had left school already.

Whether they are school records or other records—don't falsify documents! Courts are usually very familiar with the particular records they request. False records are often easy to spot and will only serve to create an additional offense.

Will I Have a Record?

Department of Motor Vehicles (DMV)

Every moving violation that isn't dismissed (either by attending traffic school or by the court) is considered a point against your driving record. Some serious offenses (e.g., reckless driving, racing, driving faster than 100 mph—check your local DMV for specifics) are considered 2 points. After you accumulate a certain number of points, the DMV may restrict or suspend your license. Understand that the DMV is a separate entity from the court and has the power to suspend your license concurrently or consecutively with the court.

The case of Josh N. illustrates the confusion that sometimes arises about concurrent or consecutive suspensions. Josh's license was suspended for ninety days by the court for speeding, and the court took possession of his license. After the suspension period expired, the court returned the license to him. Somewhere towards the end of his court suspension, however, the DMV suspended his license for another ninety days because of his point count, and the DMV sent him a letter to this effect. Josh either ignored the letter or misunderstood it, and continued to drive. He was stopped by a police officer for having tinted windows, and then cited for driving on a suspended license.

DMV points are also assigned to you if you're found "most at fault" in an accident. After every reported accident, DMV assigns percentages as to fault—for example, if it determines that one driver is 80 percent at fault and the other driver is 20 percent at fault, the first driver would be considered "most at fault," and would receive a point from DMV.

MYTH: The points I accumulate as a juvenile disappear when I turn eighteen.

MYTH BUSTER: It's not true that points you accumulate as a juvenile driver are erased when you turn eighteen. Points stay on your record for as long as they would stay if you were an adult—three, five, or ten years, depending on the offense.

Some offenses don't count as negligent driver points. These may include, for example, HOV lane violations, seatbelt tickets, and antigridlock law violations. The offenses generate fines, but no points.

The length of time an infraction stays on your DMV record varies according to state law. In California, for example, most traffic infractions, such as red light, stop sign, and speeding offenses, stay on your DMV record for three years. Other, more serious offenses—such as reckless driving, hit-and-run, and speeding over 100 mph—can stay on your record for five to ten years. Although the DMV will usually screen requests for driving records, in many states businesses can request these records as part of an employment evaluation process.

Some important terms and acronyms you might encounter when speaking to or corresponding with the DMV:

abstract: A court document specifing conviction or clearance of a failure to appear or failure to pay.

action: Having your driving privilege, certificate, or endorsement cancelled, suspended, revoked, or restricted.

conviction date: The date the court gave a ruling on the case, as reflected on the abstract of conviction.

FTA: Failure to appear in court as promised.

FTP: Failure to pay fine.

proof: Refers to proof of insurance filed with DMV by the owner and/or driver of a vehicle.

proof termination date: The date the action and the insurance filing (proof) are ended.

reinstatement date: The date the driving privilege is returned to its former status.

through (thru) term date: The date the action period is over.

violation date: The date the violation occurred, as reflected on the FTA, FTP, or abstract of conviction.

Court Records

Juvenile court records, along with legal and social records maintained by law enforcement agencies, have traditionally been kept confidential. However, as described in chapter 1, the new trend of openness in juvenile proceedings has contributed greatly to the erosion of the mandate for confidentiality. According to a 2006 report by the National Center for Juvenile Justice, delinquency hearings are open to the public in fourteen states, while twenty-one states have statutes that open delinquency hearings for some types of cases, and most states specify exceptions to juvenile court confidentiality.

Although access may be restricted to certain parts of the record and may require a court order, confidential records are now being made available to schools and agencies that serve youth as well as prosecutors, social service agencies, victims, and the public. In all states, those with "legitimate interests" may have partial access to juvenile court or law enforcement records, although interested parties must usually obtain the court's permission for that access. In addition, all states allow certain juvenile offenders to be fingerprinted and photographed, and most of these records are stored in a statewide repository. Finally, forty-four states have school notification laws, which provide that schools can be notified when students are involved with law enforcement or courts for committing some criminal acts.

Some possible consequences of having a misdemeanor on your record may include denial of a driver's license and rejection by a college or university, the armed services, or an employer.

Sealing of Juvenile Records

Sealing records is also known as **expunging** (or expunction) of records. You may request your records be sealed only after you've turned eighteen. This may involve contacting the juvenile court or the juvenile probation department in your area. The court or probation department will look at your record and make a decision as to whether the record should be sealed.

MYTH: My juvenile record will "go away" after I turn eighteen.

MYTH BUSTER: It's an urban legend that juvenile records don't count or magically "go away" after you turn eighteen. Juvenile records aren't automatically sealed upon completion of probation or at age eighteen. A petition must be filed in order to get your juvenile records sealed, and not all juvenile records may be eligible for sealing.

Juvenile Vehicle Code records stay on the record for the same amount of time as adult records. Even when a record has been sealed by the court, a partial record may remain with local police, the state bureau of criminal identification, and the FBI. Once a record has been sealed, however, the police, probation department, and court cannot legally release any information about it.

Tip

Be proactive and request that your records be sealed when you turn eighteen. Don't wait for it to happen automatically, because it probably won't.

CHAPTER 9

How to Avoid Getting Another Citation

Thanks for shining the light on me. It woke me up to really see how much everyone cares about me.

Anyone can make a mistake and receive a first citation, but multiple citations are indicative of deeper-rooted problems. There's no easy wizardry I can share with you that will guarantee you won't get another citation, but I can leave you with some words of advice. At the end of the film version of the *Wizard of Oz*, Glinda (the "good" witch) tells Dorothy, "You don't need to be helped any longer. You've always had the power." This simple statement holds true for you as well. You—and you alone—have the power within you to change your own future. There are, however, two important factors that will greatly influence whether or not you'll be in court once again: your relationships with and attitude toward your friends and family.

About Friends

I got my ticket because I was protecting one of my good friends. My friend (whose name I'm not gonna mention) did a lot for me. So she had asked me, "They are going to search me, please hold this. I'm already on probation." I feel dumb and ashamed, but it's too late already. I can't do nothing but accept my consequences.

My mom is always working and my sisters don't live with me. So I feel lonely. That's why I hang out with my friends. I'm tired of feeling alone. And I know it's not a reason, but you know what emotions make you do.

I should choose the people I surround myself with more wisely. That will be my first big step toward my long-term goal of sobriety. All of my life I have been told that I was different, that I was meant to be someone important. I am capable of things that people say are great feats. But my bad choices have put me in a situation that could easily have been avoided.

Now in this bad situation, I can definitely see the true colors of someone I thought was my friend.

Choosing your friends may be the most important decision you make in your teens. Throughout this guide, you have seen the word "friend" over and over again. That's because 90 percent of how you think and act—both good and bad—is connected with your friends. Friends also have a lot to do with whether or not you receive a citation. So consider the following:

1. A *good* friend will talk you out of doing something bad, not into it. A good friend won't suck you into doing something you wouldn't do otherwise.
2. If you don't want to bring your friend home to meet your family, chances are he is not a good friend.
3. If you don't know a person's last name, it's a sign that you probably don't know enough about her and shouldn't hang out with her.
4. Having "bad" friends usually means you don't really like yourself enough to have good friends.
5. Being a good friend doesn't always mean saying "yes." Relearn one of the first words you learned to say—"no."

6. You can't always fix your friends' problems, even if you want to. You're not equipped to handle serious boyfriend/girlfriend problems, parent problems, school problems, and drug and alcohol problems. Get an adult involved.
7. If someone's gotten you into trouble, that should be a friendship ender.
8. Having no friends is better than having bad friends.

About Siblings

I didn't realize how my actions hurt other people until I came to court, 'cause right now my brother's crying and it's my fault.

Even though I got into a lot of fights with my sister and brother, I know that, if one of them were to perish from this planet, my heart would be broken, and that would also mean I have no one to pick on anymore.

Younger or older siblings are often somchow involved in or related to a minor's citation, as in the case of Adrian R., whose sister called the police department when a gathering at Adrian's house got out of hand, or of John L., who took his younger brother along when he entered a Target store to steal a baseball cap. Siblings are an important part of your family, emotional, and legal life. So consider the following:

1. If you're an older brother or sister, act in a way that shows your younger sibling a good example.
2. Make sure your siblings don't get into trouble because of your conduct.
3. Just because you have an older sibling who's in trouble or who has been to jail, that doesn't mean that's the direction you have to take.
4. Think of you and your siblings as members of a team. Don't sit on the bench—help out whenever you can.

About Parents

How anxious parents get! How nervous, and just because of a dumb choice you made. No one exactly knows how parents feel except the parents. They must feel so embarrassed knowing that their kid was busted.

I'm so thankful I have my mom. I don't know what I would do without her. I would probably be in jail, and that's one place I don't want to go.

How would you feel if they called you from a mall saying that they have your son or daughter and that they were caught shoplifting at their store? Would you feel disappointed? Mad? Upset? Like they lost all their confidence?

I don't want my mother to have to go through the rest of her life thinking it was her fault for not raising me correctly.

Your parents are just as nervous, concerned, and worried as you are about you getting a citation and going to court. They may have their own issues—guilt or childhood experiences that relate to your behavior. People express their concerns in different ways. Some parents get mad, while others get upset and sad. Some parents will take away privileges or punish you before your court hearing. Others will wait for the outcome. Understand that it may be just as traumatic for them as it is for you. So consider the following:

1. You don't really want your parents "covering up" or lying for you. A good parent teaches you honesty by being truthful.
2. You don't want your parents rewarding you for bad behavior, such as buying you the same items you stole from a store.
3. Don't be tempted to take advantage of your divorced parents' fighting over money or custody. Don't use it as an excuse to move from household to household as a way of avoiding discipline. Don't let yourself and your problems be used by your parents as a way of "getting even" with each other.

4. It's not cool if your parents aren't interested in your grades.
5. It's a good idea to thank your parents for supporting you and making time to leave work to accompany you to court.

Finally, the best way to stay out of court, is to—

Be your own **J**udge
Understand your own motivations
Have a **V**ested interest in your community
Think about your **I**mpulses
Elect to be with good friends

And remember—I'll be rooting for you!

Resources on the Web

American Bar Association Center on Children and the Law: www.abanet.org/child

American Bar Association Children's Rights Litigation Committee: www.abanet.org/litigation/committees/childrights

Job Corps: http://jobcorps.dol.gov

National Association of Counsel for Children (NACC): www.nacchildlaw.org

National Center for Juvenile Justice: www.ncjj.org

National Council on Crime and Delinquency (NCCD): www.nccd-crc.org/nccd/n_index_main.html

National Council of Juvenile and Family Court Judges: www.ncjfcj.org

National Criminal Justice Reference Service: www.ncjrs.gov

National Juvenile Court Data Archive: http://ojjdp.ncjrs.org/ojstatbb/njcda

Office of Juvenile Justice and Delinquency Prevention (OJJDP): http://ojjdp.ncjrs.org

Public Counsel: www.publiccounsel.org

Glossary

adjudication: A juvenile court hearing in which a plea is made.

affidavit of non-liability: A written statement alleging that an individual is not responsible for an offense (usually filed in a photo red light citation).

affidavit of prejudice: A written declaration alleging prejudice on the part of the judge.

age of majority: The age at which a person legally becomes an adult.

aiding and abetting: Actively, knowingly, intentionally, or purposefully assisting someone in committing a crime.

amendment: A change made to a citation after it has been written.

appeal: A request to a higher court for the purpose of obtaining a review of the lower court's order.

arraignment: A hearing in court where the defendant appears to hear and answer the charges against him.

assault: An attempt to hurt someone physically in a way that makes him or her feel immediately threatened; physical contact isn't necessary.

average plus/minus error rate: The error rate of a law enforcement officer after he has been tested for speed estimation.

bar association: A local, statewide, or national organization of attorneys.

battery: An intentional, unlawful physical contact inflicted on a person by another without consent.

bench warrant: An arrest warrant that is issued "from the bench," i.e., by a judge.

beyond a reasonable doubt: The level of proof necessary to convict a person of a crime. It does not require 100 percent proof, but rather that there should not be any reasonable doubt as to the individual's guilt.

burden of proof: The obligation of a party (the state, in criminal cases) to prove an allegation of guilt in court.

burglary: The entry into a building or occupied structure with the purpose of committing a crime.

calibration: The checking or correction of a speedometer or radar/laser device.

certificate of correction: A certificate that must be signed by a police officer indicating that a correctable violation has been fixed.

citable offense: A violation for which a person can be summoned to court via a citation.

city attorney: The legal counsel who represents the interests of the city.

code section: The specific section or subsection of a numbered legal code or law.

consolidated cases: Cases where companion cases are heard in court together.

contested hearing: A hearing in which the allegation of a police officer is contested in court, similar to a trial in adult court.

continuance: A postponement of a hearing to a later date.

correctable violation: A violation that can be corrected before appearing in court; also known as a "fix-it" ticket.

counseled and released: Counseling by a police or probation officer at the scene of an incident or later, without formal charges.

credibility: The believability of a person's testimony or account of an incident.

cross-examine: To question a witness in order to determine truthfulness.

declarant: A person who makes a statement in writing.

de minimus: Latin for a small or unimportant matter.

dependent child: A child whose custody and control has been taken from the parents by the state (similar to "ward of the state").

detention: Being held in temporary custody at a police stop, station, or juvenile hall.

discovery request: A defendant's pretrial request for the disclosure of all pertinent information.

discretion: The freedom and authority of a judge to make decisions.

disposition: The outcome of a juvenile court proceeding, similar to "sentencing" in adult court.

district attorney: The legal counsel who represents the interests of the county.

disturbing the peace: Interrupting the peace, quiet, or good order of a community with unnecessary and distracting noises or actions.

driving out of class: Driving a vehicle (such as a motorcycle) with a driver's license that does not have the proper endorsement.

DUI: An acronym for driving under the influence of alcohol or drugs.

emancipation: Surrender of the care and custody of a minor by parents of their parental duties.

exigent circumstance: A sudden, unexpected happening, an unforeseen occurrence or condition.

expunging: Erasure of records.

extension: A postponement of a due date on a citation.

failure to appear: Failure to appear in court on the day prescribed by the citation, a separate and additional offense.

fatal flaw: A mistake on a citation that is so serious it nullifies the citation.

felony: A serious criminal offense punishable by a prison sentence of more than one year.

fine: A sum of money required to be paid as punishment or penalty for an offense.

fitness hearings: Hearings that determine whether minors are "fit" or "unfit" to be tried in adult court for serious offenses.

fix-it ticket: A citation that is designated as correctable. The fine for the offense is lowered or dismissed entirely upon proof of correction to the court.

giving false information to an officer: A separate offense for giving any untrue or misleading information to an officer during questioning including name, age, address, and so on.

good faith: A good or sincere intention, the absence of intent to deceive.

hearing room: A room in which a hearing is conducted. This can be a courtroom or another, less formal environment.

hearsay evidence: Statements made out of court.

hit-and-run: A collision between two motor vehicles or a motor vehicle and a pedestrian in which one driver leaves the scene without identifying him- or herself.

independent recollection: A recall of facts, not based on refreshing memory with notes or documents.

indicated sentence: The sentence a judge usually imposes for a particular offense.

informal adjustments: Informal proceedings with a probation or hearing officer that are not court hearings and that may result in a reprimand or warning only.

infraction: The least serious type of offense, such as traffic and pedestrian violations, for which there is no jail time.

juvenile holding tank: A place in a police station, separate from adult detainees, where juveniles are detained pending questioning or investigation.

legal guardian: An adult who has been formally given the right to make decisions on behalf of a minor.

lesser charge: An offense that is less serious than the original offense charged.

mandatory sentencing: Sentencing determined and prescribed in the law itself in which the judge is allowed no discretion.

maximum speed: The maximum speed a car may travel in certain areas, usually with regard to highways.

Miranda rights: Warnings that must be made by law enforcement to a person who has been taken into custody prior to any custodial interrogation as to their Constitutional rights.

misdemeanor: A criminal offense, less serious than a felony, punishable by a jail sentence of one year or less, such as shoplifting and trespassing.

mitigating factors: Factors considered by a judge that may lessen the seriousness of an offense or severity of the sentence.

nolo contendere: Latin for "no contest," this is a plea by which a defendant in a criminal case does not make a defense but does not admit guilt. A plea of "no contest" has the same effect as a guilty plea but cannot prejudice the defendant's case in a civil proceeding based on the same incident.

notice of civil demand: A notice claiming a legal right to an amount owed.

notice to appear: A citation or ticket is a notice to appear in court.

pacing: A means to determine the speed of a vehicle, usually involving following a vehicle at a certain distance for a certain amount of time.

penalty assessment: A surcharge imposed in addition to a fine, which can be more than double the fine outlined in a code section.

perjury: Making a false statement under oath.

petition: A request on behalf of the state, made by a district attorney, to deem a minor a delinquent ward of the state.

petty theft: The taking of property without the owner's consent, where the property is valued under a specific amount.

plea: A defendant's formal response to a criminal charge.

pleading: A formal allegation by a party as to its claims.

prima facie speed: The speed posted or designated on a traffic control sign, which may be legal to exceed if conditions are safe.

priors: A defendant's history of prior offenses.

probable cause: Reasonable cause or suspicion for an officer to stop or detain a person or vehicle.

prowling: Loitering or lingering on private property with the purpose of committing a crime.

recall of warrant: A withdrawal or revocation of a warrant for arrest.

recuse: To disqualify a judge from a hearing because of prejudice or a conflict of interest.

rehabilitation facilities: Treatment facilities where people addicted to alcohol or drugs are ordered by a court or attend voluntarily for the purpose of overcoming their addiction.

rehearing: A second hearing before a different or higher court in the case of an error, omission, or oversight.

release of liability: A written statement discharging a person from responsibility for an incident.

sealing records: The process by which a minor's criminal record is shielded from public view and thereafter cannot be examined except by court order.

self-incrimination: Statements or answers to questions, made by a person himself, that make him appear guilty of a crime or at fault.

speed estimation: The process by which an officer determines a driver's speed without the use of a laser or radar device.

speedy trial: The right of someone accused of an offense to a trial without unreasonable delay, guaranteed by the Sixth Amendment to the Constitution.

sponsor: A person who supports and guides another through a twelve-step program.

statement of rights: A written notice explaining a defendant's rights.

status offenses: Acts that are illegal if committed by a juvenile (for example, truancy, running away from home, curfew violations).

subpoena: A legal order directing a person to appear in court to give testimony or present records.

therapeutic jurisprudence: An approach to law that emphasizes mental health and social factors.

time waiver: The voluntary relinquishment of the right to a speedy trial.

traffic and engineering survey: A survey of a road conducted by a licensed traffic engineer.

trial in absentia: A trial held not in the presence of the defendant.

venue: The geographical location where a case is heard and determined. "Change of venue" refers to the removal of a case from one district or county to another.

ward: A person incapable of managing his or her own affairs and for whom the court steps in to make decisions.

Appendix
Document Examples

Citation

LOS ANGELES COUNTY SHERIFF'S DEPARTMENT

STATION

☐ MISDEMEANOR
☐ TRAFFIC
☐ NONTRAFFIC
☐ CONTINUATION FORM ISSUED

NOTICE TO APPEAR

M689631

DATE OF VIOLATION / / | TIME ☐ AM ☐ PM | DATE OF WEEK S M T W T F S | R.D.

NAME *(FIRST, MIDDLE, LAST)* ☐ OWNER'S RESPONSIBILITY (VEH. CODE, § 40001)

ADDRESS

CITY | STATE | ZIP CODE

DRIVER LIC. NO. | STATE | CLASS | AGE | BIRTH DATE / / | ☐ JUVENILE (PHONE NO.) ( )

SEX | HAIR | EYES | HEIGHT | WEIGHT | RACE | PASSENGERS

VEH. LIC. NO. OR VIN | STATE

☐ **COMMERCIAL VEHICLE** (VEH. CODE, § 15210(b))

YR. OF VEH. | MAKE | MODEL | BODY STYLE | COLOR

☐ **HAZARDOUS MATERIAL** (VEH. CODE, § 353)

EVIDENCE OF FINANCIAL RESPONSIBILITY

REGISTERED OWNER OR LESSEE ☐ SAME AS DRIVER

ADDRESS ☐ SAME AS DRIVER

CITY | STATE | ZIP CODE

CORRECTABLE VIOLATION (VEH. CODE, § 40610) ☐ BOOKING REQUIRED

YES	NO	CODE AND SECTION	DESCRIPTION	MISDEMEANOR OR INFRACTION (CIRCLE)
☐	☐			M I
☐	☐			M I
☐	☐			M I
☐	☐			M I

SPEED APPROX. | P.F./MAX. SPD. | VEH. LMT. | SAFE | RADAR | LASER | CITY

LOCATION OF VIOLATION(S)

AT

FILE# ☐ ACCIDENT

☐ VIOLATIONS NOT COMMITTED IN MY PRESENCE, DECLARED ON INFORMATION AND BELIEF.
I DECLARE UNDER PENALTY OF PERJURY UNDER THE LAWS OF THE STATE OF CALIFORNIA THE FOREGOING IS TRUE AND CORRECT.

ARRESTING OR CITING OFFICER | BADGE NO. | VAC. DATES TO

/ / DATE | NAME OF ARRESTING OFFICER, IF DIFFERENT FROM CITING OFFICER | BADGE NO. | VAC. DATES TO

WITHOUT ADMITTING GUILT, I PROMISE TO APPEAR AT THE TIME AND PLACE INDICATED BELOW

X SIGNATURE

WHEN: ON OR BEFORE THIS DATE: / / TIME: ☐ AM ☐ PM

WHAT TO DO: FOLLOW THE INSTRUCTIONS ON THE REVERSE.

WHERE: COURT LA SUPERIOR COURT-NORTH DIST

ADDRESS 1040 WEST AVENUE J

CITY LANCASTER, CA 93534

PHONE 661-945-6337

OR YOU MAY ATTEND NIGHT COURT ON / / AT PM

Notice to Appear form approved by the Judicial Council of California.
Rev. 06-15-01 (Veh. Code, §§ 40500(b), 40513(b), 40522, 40600;
Pen. Code, § 853.9) 761551 SH-CR-66

☐ NO NIGHT COURT AVAILABLE FOLLOW THE INSTRUCTIONS ON THE REVERSE

1900

Photo Red Light Ticket

Los Angeles
Metropolitan Transportation Authority
Automated Enforcement
Traffic Violation

JUVENILE

You can view full color versions of the images below at:
http://www.cite-web.com
Citation number: Pin Number:

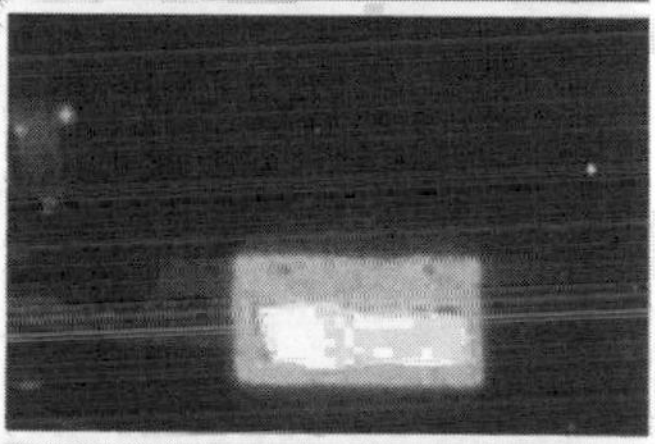

Citation No.

LOS ANGELES COUNTY SHERIFF'S DEPARTMENT
NOTICE TO APPEAR Automated Traffic Enforcement 083081TT

Date of Violation 01/02/2007	Time 21:30 [ ] AM [X] PM	Day of Week TUESDAY	Case No.

Name (First, Middle, Last)

Address

City RESEDA	State CA	Zip Code 91335

Driver Lic. No.	State CA	Class	Commercial [ ] Yes [x] No	Age 17	Birth Date 07/22/1989

Sex M	Hair Black	Eyes Black	Height 5-07	Weight 145	Race

COPY

Veh. Lic. No. or VIN	State CA

Yr. of Veh. 2005	Make HYUN	Model	Body Style 4D	Color MEDIUM

[ ] COMMERCIAL VEHICLE (Veh. Code, § 15210(b))
[ ] HAZARDOUS MATERIAL (Veh. Code, § 353)

Registered Owner or Lessee

Address

City RESEDA	State CA	Zip Code 91335

Code and Section VC 21453A	Description Fail to Stop Red Signal

Location of Violation at
SB Lindley Ave. @ Busway

* Violation was not committed in my presence. The above is declared on information and belief and is based on photographic evidence.

I declare under penalty of perjury under the laws of the State of California the foregoing is true and correct.

Date Issued	Declarant	ID No.
07/13/2007		

YOU MUST RESPOND TO THE COURT ON OR BEFORE:

WHEN: DATE: **August 17, 2007**

WHAT TO DO: FOLLOW THE INSTRUCTIONS ON THE REVERSE

WHERE: Van Nuys Informal Juvenile Traffic Court
6230 Sylmar Ave
Room 340
Van Nuys, CA 91401
Phone: 818-374-2332

Judicial Council of California Form
REV. 05-20-05 (Veh. Code, § 40518)

SEE REVERSE
TR-115

Juvenile Delinquency Petition

2007 OCT 10 PM . 16 SUPERIOR COURT SYLMAR JUVENILE

SUPERIOR COURT OF CALIFORNIA
COUNTY OF LOS ANGELES
JUVENILE COURTS

FILED
LOS ANGELES SUPERIOR COURT
OCT 10 2007
CLERK
DEPUTY

JAIN:
PDJ:
PROB: LACO PROB DEPT SYLMAR JUVENILE HALL/IDC
COMP:
DACASE:

THE PEOPLE OF THE STATE OF CALIFORNIA, Petitioner, v. Minor.	CASE NO **New** Comp: ***PETITION UNDER SECTION 602 OF THE WELFARE AND INSTITUTIONS CODE***

PETITIONER is informed and believes, and thereon alleges, that hereinafter called minor, resides at , was born on was years of age on **09/28/2007.**

The name and address of each parent and guardian of minor, if known to me, or if none is known, the name and residence address of an adult relative residing within the county, or if none is known, the name and address of the adult relative known to me to reside nearest to the court, is:

Mother

Said minor was taken into custody by **LAPD - NORTH HOLLYWOOD AREA, 10/05/2007, at 05:15 PM.** Minor **is Detained**. The present whereabouts of minor is **SYLMAR JUVENILE HALL.**

Further, that minor comes within the provisions of Section 602 of the Welfare and Institutions Code of California, in that:

COUNT 1: On or about 09/28/2007 within the County of Los Angeles, the crime of FIRST DEGREE RESIDENTIAL BURGLARY, in violation of PENAL CODE 459, a Felony, was committed by said minor, who did enter an inhabited dwelling house and trailer coach and inhabited portion of a building occupied by with the intent to commit larceny and any felony.

It is further alleged that the above offense is a violation of Penal Code Section 462(a).

COUNT 2: On or about 09/28/2007 within the County of Los Angeles, the crime of FIRST DEGREE RESIDENTIAL BURGLARY, in violation of PENAL CODE 459, a Felony, was committed by said minor, who did enter an inhabited dwelling house and trailer coach and inhabited portion of a building occupied by with the intent to commit larceny and any felony.

Police Report

STATE OF CALIFORNIA
NARRATIVE/SUPPLEMENTAL
CHP 556 (Rev. 7-90) OPI 061

* P.D.O. *

Page 3 of 4

DATE OF INCIDENT/OCCURRENCE	TIME (2400)	NCIC NUMBER	OFFICER I.D. NUMBER	NUMBER
02-16-08	2255	1900		

"X" ONE: [X] Narrative [ ] Supplemental
"X" ONE: [X] Collision Report [ ] Other:
TYPE SUPPLEMENTAL ("X" APPLICABLE): [ ] BA Update [ ] Hazardous Materials [ ] Fatal [ ] School Bus [ ] Hit and Run Update [ ] Other:

CITY/COUNTY/JUDICIAL DISTRICT	REPORTING DISTRICT/BEAT	CITATION NUMBER
MALIBU / LOS ANGELES / MALIBU	1013 / 101A/EM	

LOCATION/SUBJECT	STATE HIGHWAY RELATED
DRIVE, IN MALIBU, 94.8 FT. N. OF GRASSWOOD	[ ] Yes [X] No

I. ROADWAY DESCRIPTION

DR, IN MALIBU, IS A NORTH/SOUTH RUNNING ROADWAY, WITH 1 LANE OF TRAVEL FOR EACH DIRECTION. THIS ROADWAY HAS DIRT SHOULDERS ALONG ITS EDGES, AND IS LOCATED IN A RESIDENTIAL DISTRICT.

II. A.O.I. (AREA OF IMPACT P/1 VS. FIRE HYDRANT)

THIS COLLISION OCCURRED ON CLIFFSIDE DRIVE, IN MALIBU, APPROXIMATELY 94.8 FT. N. OF GRASSWOOD AND APPROXIMATELY 4.6 FT. E. OF THE E.C.L. OF DR.

III. STATEMENTS (P/1)

P/1 SAID, HE WAS TRAVELING E/B ON GRASSWOOD APPROACHING CLIFFSIDE DRIVE. P/1 SAID HE BELIEVES HE CAME TO A FULL STOP AT THE INTERSECTION OF GRASSWOOD AND CLIFFSIDE DR, HOWEVER HE MAY HAVE DONE A CA. ROLL (REFERRING TO THE FACT, THAT HE MAY NOT HAVE CONDUCTED A FULL/COMPLETE STOP AT A STOP SIGN). UPON REACHING THIS INTERSECTION, P/1 CONDUCTED A LEFT (N/B) TURN ONTO CLIFFSIDE DRIVE FROM GRASSWOOD. WHILE CONDUCTING THIS TURN, HE (P/1) LOST CONTROL OF HIS VEHICLE, CAUSING HIM TO EXIT THE ROADWAY, AND COLLIDE INTO A FIRE HYDRANT. HIS VEHICLE CAME TO REST ON TOP OF THE FIRE HYDRANT, WHICH WAS SPOUTING HIGH PRESSURED WATER. THE DRIVER (P/1) ATTEMPTED TO MOVE HIS VEHICLE FROM THE FIRE HYDRANT, BUT WAS UNABLE TO DO SO.

IV. DAMAGE

AS A RESULT OF P/1'S COLLISION WITH THE FIRE-HYDRANT, WATER DAMAGE OCCURRED TO P/1'S VEHICLE, AS WELL AS NUMEROUS RESIDENTS LOCATED ON THE EAST SIDE OF CLIFFSIDE DRIVE, WHICH ALL SUSTAINED WATER DAMAGE IN VARIOUS DEGREES (BOTH TO THEIR LANDSCAPING / GARAGES). THE LOCATIONS WHICH SUSTAINED WATER DAMAGE ARE LOCATED ON PG. 4 OF THIS REPORT. (SEE NEXT PG.)

[X] Continued

PREPARER'S NAME and I.D. NUMBER	DATE	REVIEWER'S NAME	DATE
	02-16-08		

Use previous editions until depleted.

OSP 04 82787

School Police Report

LASPD 05.02.1 – **RELEASE FROM CUSTODY REPORT CONTINUATION** (For use with Notice to Appear Citation)
Rev.(04/30/05)

DISTRIBUTION INSTRUCTIONS:
After this form is completed & approved, place the Notice to Appear Citation on this (left) side and photocopy required number of copies.

Forward the original Notice to Appear Citation and two copies of the entire report to the Deputy City Attorney.

COMBINED EVIDENCE REPORT:

If this RFC is used as a combined evidence report:

- Itemize and describe evidence in space provided. If space is insufficient, continue at beginning of Narrative.
- Forward copy of completed face sheet with the Evidence. (2 copies if narcotics.) **THIS IS THE RESPONSIBILITY OF THE OFFICER BOOKING THE EVIDENCE.**

NOTE: On multiple arrest, check the Combined Evid. Rpt. box on all the reports. Also enter the location booked, date booked & booked to info on all reports. Itemize the evidence on the report of the arrestee to whom the evidence is booked. Forward a copy of that report with the evidence.

Los Angeles School Police Department

RELEASE FROM CUSTODY **SPD # 07-10334**

☐ COMBINED EVID. RPT.

ITEM #, QUANTITY, DESCRIPTION

LOCATION BKD

DATE BKD

BKD TO (IF MULTI ARREST)

2007 AUG 11 AM 1 16

	NAME	DOB	ADDRESS	ZIP CODE	DAY PHONE
V-1					
W-1					
W-2					

ADMONITION OF RIGHTS BY

YOU HAVE THE RIGHT TO REMAIN SILENT. DO YOU UNDERSTAND? **Yes**

ANYTHING YOU SAY MAY BE USED AGAINST YOU IN COURT. DO YOU UNDERSTAND? **Yes**

YOU HAVE THE RIGHT TO THE PRESENCE OF AN ATTORNEY BEFORE AND DURING ANY QUESTIONING. DO YOU UNDERSTAND? **Yes**

☐ READ IN SPANISH

IF YOU CANNOT AFFORD AN ATTORNEY, ONE WILL BE APPOINTED FOR YOU, FREE OF CHARGE, BEFORE ANY QUESTIONING, IF YOU WANT. DO YOU UNDERSTAND? **Yes**

DO YOU WANT TO TALK ABOUT WHAT HAPPENED? **Yes**

PRELIMINARY DRUG TEST	TYPE OF TEST	SUPV/INV. OFCR TESTING	OFFICER WITNESSING	QUANTITY/NET WEIGHT
☐ POSITIVE ☐ INCONCLUSIVE	N/A			

NARRATIVE (ADD'L. EVID./WITS, CO-ARRESTEES, SOURCE OF ACTIVITY OBSERVATIONS, ARRESTS, RFC, EVIDENCE, ADDITIONAL)

Subject 1:

Parent:

Subject 2:

Parent:

Charges: 308(b) P.C.-Juvenile in Possession of Tobacco/ Paraphernalia.

Source of Activity:

On 08/06/07 at approximately 0820 hours, I, Officer was working for Los Angeles School Police Department in full uniform and in a marked police vehicle assigned to Reseda High School as 1J62. While patrolling the area, I observed two juveniles at Reseda Park with their backpacks loitering (during summer school hours). As soon as the juveniles saw my patrol vehicle one of the juveniles grabbed something from the bench and quickly placed the item inside his pant pocket as if he was trying to hide the item. The juveniles got up and began walking toward Reseda High School. I made contact with the juveniles to find out if they were Reseda High School students.

ID VERIFIED BY ☒ SCHOOL RECORDS ☐ CDL / ID

CLEARED BY WANTS/ WARRANT CHECK YES ☒ NO ☐

RAP SHEET ATTACHED YES ☐ NO ☒

CITATION No.

☐ JUVENILE INVOLVED PARENT (S) NAME

ADD /PH# ☒ SAME AS SUBJ.

☐ NARR. CONT

ISSUING OFCR'S PARTNER	SERIAL #	APPROVING SUPERVISOR	SERIAL #	LOCATION	LOCATION CODE
		[signature]		Reseda H.S.	8814

RFC 1.0 - 10/97-00662 (rev 04/30/05)

Department Store Juvenile Criminal Trespass Warning

Juvenile Criminal Trespass Warning

Case #: ____________ Date: 9/29/2007

I understand that for my son's / daughter's unlawful activities, my chilc ____________ is not a member of the public entitled to be in any [redacted]

I further understand that my son / daughter is not allowed to enter or remain on any premise belonging to [redacted], without parental supervision, for a period of two years.

I understand that any entry by my son / daughter into any [redacted] store during this time would be an unlawful entry which violates this agreement. Violation of this order may result in prosecution.

I have read or have had read to me the above warning. I understand that refusal to sign this warning does not relieve my son / daughter from criminal prosecution if the criminal trespass warning is violated.

Parent / Guardian Signature: ____________ Date: 9/29/2007

Witness: ____________ Date: 9/29/2007 Time: 3:pm

DL or ID # N/A

Height: 5'4

Weight: 110

Hair: brn Eyes: black

D.O.B. ____________

Notes: ____________

Probation Report

ATTORNEY'S NAME: (FIRST & LAST)	TYPE
ADDRESS:	
PHONE:	

SUPERIOR COURT OF CALIFORNIA
COUNTY OF LOS ANGELES
JUVENILE COURT

DEPT.	DATE	APP. / NON-APP.
204	11/13/2007	APPEARANCE

COURT NO.:
JAIN:
PDJ NO.:
SSN:
SID NO.:

IN THE MATTER OF:

CASE NAME (LAST, FIRST, MIDDLE)	
AKA	D.O.B.

USUALLY LIVES WITH	CURRENT WHEREABOUTS	
MOTHER	HOME	
CURRENT STATUS: 602 HOP	AREA: VAN	DPO: IG82
DPO RECOMMENDATION - CODE: 602 WIC - CAMP (Mid-Term) - 18b		

PROBATION OFFICER'S REPORT

REASON FOR HEARING:

THE MATTER WAS LAST BEFORE THE COURT ON 8/27/07 AND WAS CONTINUED TO THIS DATE FOR A SUPPLEMENTAL REPORT REGARDING MINOR'S DRUG TESTING AND SCHOOLING.

REPORT:

ON 8/27/07, THE COURT DEEMED THE PROGRESS REPORT A 777 WIC AND INFORMED THE MINOR SHOULD HE CONTINUE TO VIOLATE HIS CONDITIONS OF PROBATION HE WOULD BE ORDERED TO COMPLETE A SIX MONTH CAMP PROGRAM. IN REGARDS TO THE MINOR'S DRUG TESTING ORDER, HE WAS DRUG TESTED ON 9/13/07 AND 10/4/07 AND TESTED NEGATIVE FOR ALL DRUGS. IN THE AREA OF ACADEMICS, THE MINOR'S FIVE-WEEK PROGRESS REPORT FROM NORTH HOLLYWOOD HIGH SCHOOL INDICATED THE MINOR EARNED A "D" GRADE IN BIOLOGY AND ADV. APP. MATH. HE EARNED A "FAILING " GRADE IN INTRO COMPUTERS AND PRINCIPLE AMERICAN DEMOCRACY. MINOR ALSO HAD NUMEROUS ABSENCES IN ALL SIX CLASSES (PLEASE SEE ATTACHED

Juvenile Conditions of Probation Form

JUVENILE CONDITIONS OF PROBATION

(Check Conditions Being Recommended)

1. ☐ Obey all laws. Obey all orders of the Probation Officer and of any court.
2. ☐ __ Obey all instructions and orders of ☐ Parents/Guardians ☐ Teacher(s) ☐School Officials ☐ Other ____.
3. ☐ Report to the Probation Officer as directed.
4. ☐ __ Notify the Probation Officer before changing address, school, school schedule or place of employment.
5. ☐ Seek and maintain training or employment as directed by the Probation Officer.
6. ☐ __ Do not engage in ____.
7. ☐ Do not leave camp or suitable placement without permission.
8. ☐ __ Perform 80 hours of work under the supervision of the Probation Officer.
9. ☐ Attend a school program approved by the Probation Officer. Maintain satisfactory grades and attendance, and citizenship. Promptly notify Probation Officer of every absence.
12. ☐ __ Do not be within one block of any school ground unless enrolled, attending classes, on approved school business, or with school official, parent or guardian.
13. ☐ Do not be out of residence between ____ and ____ except with parental consent.
14. ☐ __ Do not stay away from residence for more than 24 hours, nor leave Los Angeles County except at times and places specifically permitted in advance by the Probation Officer.
15. ☐ Do not associate with ☐ co-minors ☐ anyone disapproved of by ☐ Parent ☐ Probation Officer ☐ Other ____
15a. ☐ __ Do not participate in any type of gang activity.
16. ☐ Do not have any dangerous or deadly weapon in your possession, nor remain in the presence of any unlawfully armed person
17. ☐ __ Do not contact or cause any contact with, nor associate with the victim(s) or witness(es) of any offense alleged against you.
18. ☐ Do not associate with children under ____ years except in presence of a responsible adult.
19. ☐ __ Do not drink any alcoholic beverages.
20. ☐ Cooperate in a plan to control abuse of alcohol, controlled substances or poisons.
21. ☐ __ Do not use or possess narcotics, controlled substances, poisons, or related paraphernalia; stay away from places where users congregate.
21a. ☐ Do not own, use or possess an electronic paging device.
22. ☐ __ Do not associate with persons known to be users or sellers of narcotics/controlled substances, except with the prior written permission of the Probation Officer.
23. ☐ Submit to urinalysis and skin checks as directed by the Probation Officer to detect the use of narcotics/controlled substances.
24. ☐ __ Submit to testing of blood, breath or urine to detect the use of alcohol, narcotics/controlled substances or poisons whenever requested by any peace officer.
25. ☐ Submit person, residence or property under your control to search and seizure at any time of the day or night by any law enforcement officer with or without a warrant. [§ 790.4 WIC]
26. ☐ __ Cooperate in a plan for psychiatric/psychological testing or treatment.
27. ☐ Pay $____ fine to the general fund of the county through the Probation Officer in such manner as the Probation Officer shall order; plus penalty assessment and surcharge (1464 Penal Code and 76000 Government Code).
28. ☐ __ Make reparation on all related losses as determined by the Probation Officer, including a service charge as authorized by 276(c) WIC.
28a. ☐ Make restitution to the Restitution Fund in the amount of $ ____ (no VICTIM LOSS).
29. ☐ __ Do not drive a motor vehicle unless licensed and properly insured as required by law.
30. ☐ Do not drive any motor vehicle.
31. ☐ __ Do not drive a motor vehicle except to and from ☐ school ☐ work.
32. ☐ Surrender operator's license to the court clerk, who shall comply with Section 13352 V.C.
33. ☐ __ Do not use any name other than ____; do not possess or display any identification in any other name.
34. ☐ Do not have blank checks in possession; do not write any portion of any check; do not have bank account upon which you may draw checks; do not use or possess any credit card.
36. ☒ __ Participate in a program of counseling with or without Parent/Guardian.
37. ☐ Minor's parents are ordered, pursuant to 727 WIC, to complete ten class sessions of a Parent education program on or before __ __ and file proof of completion with Probation.
38. ☐ __ Spend not less than ____ days nor more than ____ days in Juvenile Hall.
39. ☐ Participate in the Juvenile Alternative Work Services Program for a period of 20 days.
40. ☐ Other ____.
41. ☐ Participate in after school and weekend tutorial, vocational and recreational activities as directed by Probation Officer.
42. ☐ __ Participate in the High School Graduate/GED/WIN program and make continuing progress towards completion of high school.
43. ☐ Conditions of Probation as ordered on ____ remain in full force and effect except where modified herein.
44. ☐ Register with the local law enforcement agency in the county in which you reside, within 10 days. [§186.32]
45. ☐ Do not possess any lighters, matches, or other incendiary devices ☐ Do not possess any spray cans, markers or other marking devices.
46. ☐ Report to Juvenile Hall for ☐ Medical exam ☐ DNA testing on ____. ☐ Central (East Los Angeles) ☐ Nidorf (San Fernando) ☐ Los Padrinos (Downey)

Index

ABA (American Bar Association), 42
ADHD drugs, 100
affidavit of prejudice, 42–43
age of majority, 1
alcohol: characteristics of, 98; court-ordered classes on, 126–27; DUI, 76–77; possession of, 101–3; using, 97–100
American Bar Association (ABA), 42
anger management, 133
appeals, 60
arraignments, 53–55
arrests, 12, 15. *See also* citations
arrivals at court, 46
attention deficit hyperactivity disorder (ADHD) drugs, 100
attorneys, 42, 51

BAC (blood alcohol content), 76–77
bailiffs, 48, 51
Balanced and Restorative Justice (BARJ), 2
behavior modification programs, 133–34
bench warrants, 27
bicycle offenses, 86–87
blood alcohol content (BAC), 76–77
body language, 47–49
boot camps, 139
braking distances, 78, 79
burden of proof, 57

campfires, 119
caravanning, 78–79
carpool lanes, 82–83
cars: buying, 62, 64; child seats for, 81–82; illegal modifications to, 83; mechanical problems as defense, 71–72; proof of nonownership, 36–37. *See also* driver's licenses; driving
cell phones and driving, 83
change of venue, 55
character references, 30–31
child car seats, 81–82
child welfare laws, 2–3
cigarette use/possession, 103–4
citations: alterations to, 20; example, *166*; forgeries, 38–39; information on, 17–19; mistakes, 21–22; parents and, 16–17; probable cause and, 13–14; signing, 16; written compared to verbal, 19–20. *See also* status offenses
city attorneys, 51
civil fines, 115–16

classes, court-ordered, 124–25, 126–27, 135
clerks in court, 48, 50–51
cocaine, 99
code sections on citations, 20, 21
college acceptance, 31
community service, 125–26
companion cases, 47
compassionate use laws, 101–3
compliance with court orders, 141–43
computer offenses, 120
conditions of probation form, *173*
confidentiality, 7–8, 145–47
conflicts of interest, 43
consolidated cases, 47
continuances, 26–27
cops. *See* police officers
correctable violations, 35–36, 37
counselors/counseling, 51, 129–31
court appearances: arraignments, 53–55; arriving for, 46; attorneys, 42; consolidated cases, 47; dates/times, 25–29; demeanor at, 47–49; employees of the court, 50–53; failure to appear, 27; judge replacements, 42–43; materials to bring to, 29–38; parents/legal guardians at, 39–42, 49–50; statement of rights, 46–47. *See also* trials
court order compliance, 141–43. *See also* dispositions
court records, 7–8, 145–47
courtroom descriptions, 47
courts, types of, 4–6
credibility in citations, 21
criminal trespass warning, 116
crosswalk offenses, 85
curfew laws, 93–97

death statistics and driving, 80–81
defenses: for photo red light violations, 75; for speeding, 69–71; for stop sign violations, 71–72
demeanor in court, 47–49
Department of Motor Vehicles (DMV) violations, 143–45
Department Store Juvenile Criminal Trespass Warnings, *171*
detention, 15. *See also* stops by officers
diagrams for court, 56–57
directions, geographic, 79
discovery requests, 22
dismissal of cases, 59
dispositions: classes, 124–25, 126–27, 135; community service, 125–26; counseling, 129–31; discretion in, 121–22; diversion programs, 133–34, 137–39; driver's license changes, 122–23; drug tests, 127–28; essay writing, 129; guilty plea and, 54–55; monetary orders, 124, 125, 136; movement restrictions, 136–37; participatory programs, 131–34; prior records and, 122; "rehab," 128–29
district attorneys, 51
disturbing the peace, 113–14
diversion programs, 133–34, 137–39
DMV (Department of Motor Vehicles) violations, 143–45
document examples: citation, *166*; conditions of probation form, *173*; petition, *168*; photo red light ticket, *167*; police report, *169*; probation reports, *172*; school police report, *170*; trespass warnings, *171*
documents for court, 29–30, 56–57
"don't associate" orders, 136
dress requirements for court, 47–49
driver's licenses: bringing to court, 34; driving without, 62–66; falsification of, 66–67; permits

and, 79–80; restrictions, 80–81, 122–23; revocations, 123; suspensions, 122
driving: motorcycles, 65; motorized scooters, 87; moving violations, 143–45; recklessness, 73–79, 82–85; speeding, 67–71, 72–73; stop sign violations, 71–72; under the influence, 76–77. *See also* cars
drug courts, 5
drug paraphernalia, 103
drugs: characteristics of, 99–100; court-ordered classes, 126–27; DUI, 76–77; possession of, 101–4; tests for, 31–32, 127–28; using, 97–100
DUI (driving under the influence), 76–77

education. *See* classes, court-ordered; schools
egg throwing, 109–10
electronic monitoring, 138
emancipated minors, 40–41
emergencies: driving without a license, 64; headsets/loud music and, 84; speeding and, 70; yielding in, 77–78
employees of the court, 50–53
employment, proof of, 32
equipment violations on vehicles, 83
essay-writing, 129
estimation of speed, 69
exhibition of speed, 73
exigent circumstances, 64
expunction of records, 146–47
extensions of court orders, 142. *See also* continuances

failure to appear, 27, 59
fake identifications, 66–67
falsification of records, 143
family interventions, 31–32
fare evasion, 118–19
fatal flaws in citations, 21
federal laws, 2–3, 4
felonies, 19, 76
fights, 111–14
fines, 123, 124
fire alarms, 119
fires, 119
fireworks, 119
fitness hearings, 6–7
fix-it tickets, 35–36
flow of traffic, 69
following too closely, 78–79
formal probation, 138
foster care, 41–42
friends, choices of, 149–51

gangs, 105, 107, 108
GDL (graduated driver licensing), 80–81
glossary, 157–63
golf cart driving, 65
grace periods, 26–27
graduated driver licensing (GDL), 80–81
graffiti, 106–9
guardians, 39–40, 41–42
guilty plea, 53–55

habitual truants, 92
hate crimes, 112–13
headsets, 84
hearsay evidence, 56
high-occupancy vehicles (HOV), 82–83
history of juvenile court, 3–4
hit-and-run, 75–76
home confinement, 137–38
HOV (high-occupancy vehicles), 82–83

incarceration, 138–39
indicated sentence, 54
infractions, 19
inhalants, 100

In re Gault, 3
In re Gladys R, 13–14
In re Winship, 3
instruction permits, 79–80
insurance, proof of, 38
intent as defense, 70–71
Internet offenses, 120
Internet resources, 5, 155
interpreters, 52–53
intervention alternatives, 5–6

JJDPA (Juvenile Justice and Delinquency Prevention Act), 4
job corps, 31
joint custody, 16–17
judges, 33–34, 52
juries, 52
Juvenile Delinquency Petitions, *168*
juvenile hall, 138–39
Juvenile Justice and Delinquency Prevention Act (JJDPA), 4
Juvenile Vehicle Code records, 147
"Juvie," 151

Kent v. United States, 3
knife possession, 110–11

laser devices, 67–68
law enforcement officers. *See* police officers
laws, 2–3, 4, 146
learner's permits, 79–80
leaving the scene, 77
legal guardians, 39–40
legislation, 2–3, 4, 146
letters: to court, 26–27; to judges, 33–34, 49–50; from mechanics, 36; to victims, 34
licenses. *See* driver's licenses
life skills classes, 134
littering, 87
loitering, 105
long-term rehabilitation, 128–29
lookouts, 107–9
lost property, 117–18

marijuana, 99, 101–3
maximum speed, 67
McKeiver v. Pennsylvania, 3
MDMA, 99
mechanics, letters from, 36
medical marijuana laws, 101–3
methamphetamines, 99
military papers, 31
minors, defined, 1–2
Miranda rights, 13, 14
misdemeanors, 19, 76
mistakes on citations, 21–22
mitigating factors, 29–30
monetary court orders, 124, 125, 136
monitoring, electronic, 138
morgue programs, 131–32
motorcycle driving, 65
motorized scooters, 87
moving violations, 143–45
music, loud, 84

National Center for Juvenile Justice (NCJJ) Web site, 5
National Highway Traffic Safety Agency (NHTSA), 80–81
National Institute on Drug Abuse, 100
NCJJ (National Center for Juvenile Justice) Web site, 5
NHTSA (National Highway Traffic Safety Agency), 80–81
no contest plea, 53–55
nolo contendere, 53–55
non-contact hit-and-run, 76
notices of civil demand, 115–16
notices to appear. *See* citations

offenses. *See* status offenses
oxycodone HCL, 99

pacing, 69
paraphernalia, drug, 103
parenting classes for juveniles, 135
parents: in court, 39–40, 49–50; informing, 16–17; parenting classes for, 135; reactions of, 152–53
park trespassing, 106
parties, crashing, 106
pedestrian tickets, 85
penalty assessments, 124, 125, 136
perjury, 56
petitions, *168*
photographic evidence, 56–57, 72
photo red light tickets, 74–75, *167*
placements, 138
pleas, 53–55
points (moving violations), 143
police officers: not appearing in court, 59; pursuits by, 96; reactions to, 10–12; reports of, 22–23, 23–24, *169, 170*; trial testimony of, 57; written citations and, 19–20
possession: of alcohol/drugs, 101–4; of vandalism tools, 107–10
pre-hearing contracts, 28–29
prejudice, affidavit of, 42–43
prescription drugs, 100
prima facie speed, 67
prior records, 122
prison, 139
probable cause, 12–13
probation forms, *173*
probation officers, 51
probation reports, 142–43, *172*
progressive sanctions, 137–39
proof: burden of, 57; of correction, 35–36; of employment/volunteer work, 32; of forged citation, 38–39; of insurance, 38
prosecution, 51
prowling offenses, 105–6
punishment and rehabilitation, 6–7, 121–22
purpose of juvenile court, 2–4

racial tension, 113, 132–33
radar devices, 67–68
reckless driving, 73–79, 82–85
records, juvenile, 122, 143–47
red lights, 74–75
rehabilitation: confidentiality and, 7–8; facilities for, 128–29; punishment and, 6–7, 121–22
release of liability, 37
remorse, 49
reports: of police, 22–23, 23–24, *169, 170*; for probation, *172*; of witnesses, 23
resistance to arrest, 12, 15
responsibility, taking, 123, 124
restitution, 136
riding, unlawful, 82
rights, statements of, 46–47
right to appeal, 60
rubbernecking, 113
running away from home, 27–28

sample documents. *See* document examples
school police reports, *170*
schools: campus loitering, 105; court orders and, 125, 142; liaisons in, 51; notification laws, 146; records from, 30–31; rules violations, 92. *See also* classes, court-ordered
sealing of court records, 146–47
seatbelts, 81
self-defense, 113
sentencing phase. *See* dispositions
shoplifting, 114–17
sibling relationships, 151
sidewalk blocking, 87–88

skateboarding offenses, 85–86
smoking awareness classes, 127
speeding, 67–71, 72–73
speedometer calibrations, 37, 69–70
speedy trials, 55
Standard Juvenile Court Act, 2, 7
state courts, 4–5, 8
statements of rights, 46–47
statistics on teenage drivers, 80–81
status offenses: alcohol/drug possession, 101–4; alcohol/drug use, 97–100; computer crimes, 120; curfew violations, 93–97; defined, 89; failure to appear, 27, 59; fare evasion, 118–19; fights, 111–14; fires, 119; knife possession, 110–11; property-related (lost, stolen, or illegal), 114–18, 120; school rules violations, 92; trespassing, 104–5, 116; truancy, 89–92; vandalism, 106–10
"stay away" orders, 136
stolen property, 118
stopping distances, 78, 79
stops by officers, 9–15
stop signs, 71–72
"Straight Talk" programs, 134
street racing, 72–73
street sales, 120
stress and speeding, 70
stress management programs, 133

taggers, 106–9
tailgating, 78–79
"talking smack," 111
teen court, 5–6
temporary guardians, 41–42
text messaging and driving, 83
thefts, 114–17, 118
therapeutic jurisprudence, 7
therapists/therapy, 32–33, 129–31
thinking distances, 78, 79
"three strikes" law, 7
tickets. *See* citations
time waivers, 55
tobacco use/possession, 103–4
tolerance programs, 132–33
traffic collision reports, 23–24
traffic school, 124–25
"trash talk," 111
trespassing offenses, 104–5, 116
trespass warnings, *171*
trials: appeals, 60; continuances, 58–59; by declaration, 28; evidence to bring to, 56–57, 67–68; failure to appear, 59; purposes of, 55–56; witnesses, 57–58. *See also* court appearances
truancy, 89–92
truth telling, 56

unlawful riding offenses, 82
unsafe lane changes, 74
U.S. v. Puerta, 13

vandalism, 106–10
Vanessa's Law, 66
vehicles. *See* cars; driving
venue, change of, 55
victims, letters to, 34
volunteer activities, 32

warrantless searches, 137
warrants, bench, 27
weather conditions and driving, 84–85
Web resources, 5, 155
witnesses, 23, 42, 57–58

yielding to emergency vehicles, 77–78

About the Author

Leora Krygier has been a referee with the Los Angeles Superior Court, Juvenile Division, for almost twenty years and was profiled in the *Los Angeles Times* for her innovative use of essay writing in sentencing predelinquent teens. In her capacity in the juvenile court system, she's been a strong advocate of therapeutic justice for juveniles and has used essay writing as a way to engage and encourage teens in their own rehabilitation.

She is the author of *When She Sleeps*, selected by the New York Public Library as one of the Best Books for the Teen Age, 2005. The novel is about two teenage half-sisters separated during the Vietnam War who find one another by dreaming each other's dreams. The novel received a rave review from *Newsweek* for its "luminous prose that transports the reader." Krygier is also the author of *First the Raven*, a novel about the redeeming power of an unlikely friendship between an elderly Holocaust survivor and an Israeli former paratrooper, whose troubled daughter is implicated in a shooting.

Having worked with teens for most of her career, Krygier believes that coming of age is not a onetime event in a person's life but rather a continuous lifelong process. She enjoys writing several blogs. She lives in Los Angeles with her husband, two children, a very wise, apricot poodle named Kobi, and the sixteen-year-old inside her who sometimes refuses to completely grow up. Visit www.leorakrygier.com for more on the author.